Mediterranean Diet Cookbook for Beginners

1900+ Days of Quick, Easy Recipes for Healthy Eating and Weight Management, Including Stress-Free Dishes and a Comprehensive 4-Week Meal Plan and Prep Guide

AMBER BOURN

Disclaimer:

The recipes and information found in this book are intended for informational purposes only. While the author and publisher have used their best efforts in preparing this book, they make no representations or warranties concerning the accuracy or completeness of the contents and specifically disclaim any implied warranties of merchantability or fitness for a particular purpose. The designs and strategies contained herein may not be suitable for every situation.

This book is not intended as a substitute for the advice of a healthcare professional. If you require professional medical advice, please consult a competent healthcare professional before trying any of the recipes presented in this book.

The author and publisher are not liable for any loss of profit or other commercial damages, including, but not limited to, special, incidental, consequential, or other damages.

For diet and nutritional information based on your personal needs, it is recommended to consult with a qualified dietician.

TABLE OF CONTENTS

A LIST FOR A FUTURE GENERATION

Understand the Basics of Mediterranean Cuisine:
Familiarize yourself with the core ingredients that define this diet, such as olive oil, fresh herbs, vegetables, grains, and seafood.

Stock Your Pantry:
Ensure your kitchen is stocked with essential Mediterranean ingredients such as olives, capers, spices, and legumes to easily whip up recipes.

Learn Key Techniques:
Master basic Mediterranean cooking methods, such as grilling, roasting, and sautéing, to build a solid foundation.

Incorporate Seafood:
Learn how to select, clean, and cook various types of seafood, a staple in many Mediterranean dishes.

Explore Regional Variations:
Mediterranean cuisine varies greatly from region to region—explore dishes from Italy, Greece, Morocco, and more to appreciate its diversity.

Adapt Recipes to Your Taste:
Don't be afraid to substitute ingredients or adjust seasonings to suit your taste and dietary needs while maintaining the spirit of the cuisine.

Focus on Fresh and Seasonal Ingredients:
Emphasize using fresh and locally sourced produce to capture the essence of Mediterranean cooking.

Practice Healthy Eating Habits:
Emulate the Mediterranean lifestyle, which focuses on what you eat and how you eat—enjoy meals slowly and socially.

Utilize Herbs and Spices:
Get comfortable using a variety of herbs and spices to add flavor without the fat—basil, rosemary, thyme, cumin, and coriander are all central to the flavor profiles.

Document Your Cooking:
Keep a journal of the recipes you try, notes on what you changed, and what you would do differently next time. This will help you improve and personalize your cooking over time.

Cook with Others:
Share the cooking experience with friends or family to make the process more enjoyable and learn from each other.

A JOURNEY TO HEALTH: DISCOVERING THE MEDITERRANEAN DIET

Overview

The Mediterranean diet is renowned as a dietary plan and a sustainable lifestyle embraced by people living along the Mediterranean coast. Its primary appeal is to promote longevity and reduce the risk of chronic diseases. Heart health is notably improved due to the diet's emphasis on heart-healthy fats and high-fiber foods. The diet promotes better weight management and mental health through balanced and diverse nutritional intake.

Regional Influences

The Mediterranean diet varies subtly across different regions, each adding its cultural flair to the core principles:

Southern Italy: The diet is heavy on vegetables, pasta, and fish and uses olive oil as the primary fat. Tomatoes, a central ingredient, are used extensively, fresh and cooked.

Greece: The Greek variant is abundant in fruits and vegetables, grains, olive oil, and a moderate amount of fish and poultry. Dairy is primarily consumed in the form of cheese and yogurt.

The Levant: This area incorporates many legumes, fruits, and whole grains. The cuisine is rich in flavors, using herbs and spices like mint, parsley, and garlic.

North Africa: Influenced by both the Arab culinary landscape and the Mediterranean, this region utilizes spices like cinnamon and nutmeg and relies heavily on grains like couscous.

Essential Ingredients

Pantry Staples: The staples of the Mediterranean pantry reflect a diet rich in diversity and flavor:

Oils: Extra virgin olive oil is crucial, used not just for cooking but also as a dressing.

Grains: Freekeh, bulgur, and couscous are popular, alongside more familiar whole grains like oats and pasta.

Proteins: Fish such as salmon and tuna are staples, along with plant proteins from beans, chickpeas, and lentils.

Spices and Herbs: Basil, thyme, pepper, and sea salt are essential for adding flavor without the fat.

Shopping Tips

When shopping for Mediterranean ingredients, focus on freshness and authenticity. Fresh, local catches are best for seafood, but well-sourced frozen fish can also be suitable.

Basic Techniques & Cooking Methods

Grilling and Broiling: Perfect for fish, meats, and vegetables, adding flavor without fat.

Roasting: Enhances vegetables and meats' natural flavors ss without excessive seasoning.

Sautéing: This method is quick and efficient for vegetables and proteins. It uses a small amount of oil over medium-high heat.

CLASSIC HUMMUS

Servings: 8, Prep Time: 15 minutes, Cook Time: 0 minutes

2 cups canned chickpeas, drained, reserve
1/4 cup liquid
1/3 cup tahini
1/4 cup extra virgin olive oil
3 tbsp lemon juice
2 cloves garlic, minced
1/2 tsp ground cumin
Salt, to taste

1. Rinse and remove loose skins from chickpeas for smoother hummus.
2. In a food processor, combine chickpeas, tahini, olive oil, lemon juice, garlic, and cumin; blend until smooth.
3. Gradually add reserved chickpea liquid for the desired consistency.
   Season with salt and optional spices.
4. Garnish with optional items, and drizzle olive oil on top.
5. Chill for at least 30 minutes before serving for enhanced flavor.
   Per Serving: Calories: 200, Protein: 6g, Carbs: 12g, Fat: 15g, Fiber: 4g, Sodium: 300mg (varies).

MARINATED OLIVES

Servings: 8, Preparation Time: 10 minutes, Cook Time: 0 minutes, Marinating Time: At least 12 hours

2 Cups mixed olives
1/4 cup extra virgin olive oil
Zest of 1 orange
Zest of 1 lemon
2 cloves garlic, thinly sliced
2 tbsp fresh rosemary, chopped
1 tbsp fresh thyme leaves
2 bay leaves

1. Rinse olives if too salty, then drain.
2. Mix olives, olive oil, citrus zests, garlic, herbs, pepper flakes, and bay leaves. If using balsamic vinegar, add it.
3. Transfer to an airtight container, seal, and shake to coat.
4. Refrigerate for at least 12 hours, shaking occasionally for even marination.
   Per Serving: Calories: 150, Protein: 0.8g, Carbs: 3g, Fat: 15g, Fiber: 2g, Sodium: ~400mg.

STUFFED GRAPE LEAVES (DOLMAS)

Servings: 6: Prep Time: 30 minutes Cook Time: 45 minutes

60 grape leaves, jarred or fresh
1 cup uncooked long-grain rice
1/3 cup olive oil
1 large onion
1/4 cup pine nuts
1/2 cup fresh herbs
2 tbsp dried mint
1 tsp ground cinnamon
1/2 tsp allspice
2 lemons, juiced
Salt and pepper
2 cups vegetable broth

1. Rinse jarred leaves or blanch fresh leaves for 3-4 minutes. Drain.
2. Sauté onion and nuts in olive oil until golden. Add rice, currants, herbs, cinnamon, allspice, dried mint, salt, and pepper; cook for 5 minutes. Add half the lemon juice; cook 2 minutes.
3. Place a spoonful of filling on each leaf, fold over the edges, and roll tightly.
4. Place rolls seam-side down in a pot. Cover with broth, remaining lemon juice, and a drizzle of olive oil. Place a plate on top to keep it submerged. Simmer covered, 45 minutes.

Per serving: Calories: 240, Protein: 4g, Carbs: 31g, Fat: 12g, Fiber: 4g, Sodium: 400mg.

BRUSCHETTA WITH TOMATO AND BASIL

Servings: 6 servings, Prep Time: 15 minutes, Cook Time: 5 minutes

Slices of rustic whole-grain bread
3 large ripe tomatoes
1 cup fresh basil
1/4 cup olive oil
2 cloves garlic
1 tbsp balsamic vinegar

1. Salt and freshly ground black pepper
2. Toast slices under the broiler or in a toaster until crispy. Rub with garlic.
3. Mix tomatoes, basil, mozzarella (if using), garlic, olive oil, vinegar, salt, and pepper. Let sit for 5-10 minutes.
4. Top each slice with tomato mixture, ensuring juices are included.
5. Drizzle with olive oil and garnish with basil. If desired, add red pepper flakes or olives.

Per Serving: Calories: 180, Protein: 6g, Carbs: 18g, Fat: 9g, Fiber: 3g, Sodium: 200mg.

FALAFEL

Servings: 6 (18-20 falafel balls), Prep Time: 15 minutes (plus 8 hours soaking), Cook Time: 30 minutes

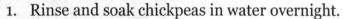

2 cups dried chickpeas
1 small onion, chopped
4 cloves garlic, minced
1/2 cup fresh parsley
1/4 cup fresh cilantro
1 tsp ground cumin

1 tsp ground coriander
1/4 tsp cardamom
Salt and black pepper
1 tsp baking powder
4-6 tbsp flour
Avocado oil for frying

1. Rinse and soak chickpeas in water overnight.
2. Drain chickpeas and blend with onion, garlic, parsley, cilantro, spices, salt, and pepper until coarsely ground.
3. Mix in baking powder and flour. Let it rest for 15-30 minutes. If the mixture is too wet, add more flour.
4. Shape into golf ball-sized rounds.
5. Heat oil to 350°F and fry falafel until golden (about 4-5 minutes). Drain on paper towels.
Per Serving: Calories: 295, Protein: 13g, Carbs: 45g, Fat: 6g, Fiber: 8g, Sodium: 300mg

HEALTHY AND DELICIOUS: SLICED APPLES WITH PEANUT BUTTER

Servings: 2 servings, Prep Time: 5 minutes, Cook Time: 0 minutes

2 large apples (Fuji, Honeycrisp, Gala), cored and sliced
4 tbsp natural peanut butter
Optional toppings: Cinnamon, honey, chopped nuts (almonds, walnuts), chia seeds

1. Wash, core, and slice apples.
2. Place peanut butter in a bowl. Soften if needed by stirring or briefly warming.
3. Sprinkle apples with cinnamon, drizzle with honey, and add nuts or chia seeds.
Per Serving: Calories: 280, Protein: 8g, Carbs: 34g, Fat: 16g, Fiber: 6g, Sodium: 100mg.

SPANAKOPITA

Servings: 6, Prep Time: 20 minutes, Cook Time: 30 minutes

1 lb (450 g) fresh spinach
2 tbsp olive oil
1 large onion
2 cloves garlic, minced
1/2 cup fresh dill or parsley
4 green onions, thinly sliced

8 oz (225 g) feta cheese
2 eggs, lightly beaten
Salt and black pepper
1/4 tsp grated nutmeg (optional)
10 sheets of phyllo pastry, thawed
1/2 cup unsalted butter

1. Sauté onion and garlic in olive oil until soft. Add spinach until wilted. Drain and cool. Mix spinach with dill, green onions, feta, eggs, seasoning, and nutmeg.
2. Preheat oven to 375°F (190°C). Brush a 9x13-inch dish with butter. Layer 5 phyllo sheets, brushing each with butter. Spread filling. Top with 5 more phyllo sheets, brushing each, including the top.
3. Score the top phyllo layers. Bake for 30 minutes or until golden.
   Per Serving: Calories: 350, Protein: 14g, Carbs: 28g, Fat: 22g, Fiber: 3g, Sodium: 650mg.

SMALL SERVING OF CHEESE WITH WHOLE GRAIN CRACKERS

Service: 4 servings, Prep Time: 5 minutes, Cook Time: 0 minutes

4 oz (115 g) cheese (feta, mozzarella, aged cheddar)
16 whole-grain crackers
Optional: Fresh herbs (rosemary, thyme)
Optional: Mixed seeds (pumpkin, sunflower)
Optional: Honey or dried fruits (cranberries, apricots)

1. Slice or crumble cheese into bite-sized pieces. Use a scoop for soft cheeses like mozzarella.
2. Place crackers and cheese on a serving platter. Garnish with herbs, seeds, honey, or dried fruits for flavor and texture.
   Per Serving: Calories: 200, Protein: 7g, Carbs: 18g, Fat: 12g, Fiber: 3g, Sodium: 320mg.

OLIVE TAPENADE

Servings: 8 servings (approximately 2 cups total), Prep Time: 10 minutes, Cook Time: 0 minutes

1 cup pitted Kalamata olives
1 cup pitted green olives
2 tbsp capers, rinsed and drained
4 anchovy fillets (optional)
2 cloves garlic, minced
1/4 cup extra virgin olive oil
2 tbsp lemon juice
1 tsp fresh thyme leaves (or 1/2 tsp dried)
1/4 tsp black pepper
Optional: 1 tbsp chopped parsley, 1/2 tsp red pepper flakes

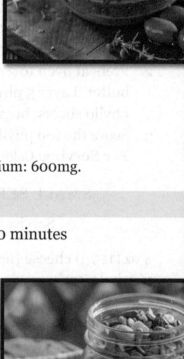

1. In a food processor, pulse olives, capers, anchovies, and garlic to chop roughly
2. Include olive oil, lemon juice, thyme, pepper, and any optional items.
3. Aim for finely chopped, with some texture.
4. Chill for at least an hour to blend flavors.
   Per Serving: Calories: 130, Protein: 1g, Carbs: 3g, Fat: 13g, Fiber: 1.5g, Sodium: 600mg.

HOMEMADE TRAIL MIX

Servings: 8 servings, Prep Time: 10 minutes, Cook Time: 0 minutes

1/2 cup raw almonds
1/2 cup walnuts
1/4 cup pistachios
1/4 cup sunflower seeds
1/4 cup pumpkin seeds

1/2 cup dried apricots, chopped
1/2 cup dried figs
1/4 cup raisins or dried cranberries

1. Combine all nuts and seeds in a large bowl.
2. Incorporate apricots, figs, and raisins/cranberries.
3. Sprinkle with cinnamon, cocoa, and sea salt.
4. Keep in an airtight container at room temp for 2 weeks or refrigerate for a month.
   Per Serving: Calories: 250, Protein: 6g, Carbs: 20g, Fat: 18g, Fiber: 4g, Sodium: 10mg.

SALADS

CHICKPEA AND AVOCADO SALAD

Servings: 4 servings, Prep Time: 15 minutes, Cook Time: 0 minutes

1 can (15 oz) chickpeas
2 ripe avocados
1/2 red onion
1 cucumber
1/2 cup cherry tomatoes

1/4 cup fresh parsley
1/4 cup fresh cilantro
Juice of 1 lemon
3 tablespoons olive oil
Salt and black pepper

1. Combine chickpeas, avocados, red onion, cucumber, and cherry tomatoes in a large bowl.
2. Include parsley, cilantro, and, if desired, cumin or chili flakes.
3. Whisk lemon juice, olive oil, salt, and pepper. Adjust seasoning to taste.
4. Pour dressing over salad and toss gently. Chill for 10 minutes to meld flavors or serve immediately.
    Per serving: Calories: 280 kcal, Protein: 7 g, Carbohydrates: 20 g, Fat: 20 g, Fiber: 8 g, Cholesterol: 0 mg, Sodium: 300 mg, Potassium: 700 mg

QUINOA WITH CHERRY TOMATOES, CUCUMBERS, FETA CHEESE, AND OLIVES

Servings: 4, Prep Time: 15 minutes, Cook Time: 15 minutes

1 cup quinoa
(uncooked)
2 cups water
1 cup cherry
tomatoes
1 cucumber
1/2 cup olives

1/2 cup feta cheese
1/4 cup red onion
1/4 cup fresh parsley
3 tablespoons extra
virgin olive oil
Juice of 1 lemon
Salt and pepper

1. Rinse the quinoa and boil it in 2 cups water. Simmer for 15 minutes.
2. In a large bowl, Prepare the tomatoes, cucumber, olives, onion, and parsley.
3. Whisk olive oil, lemon juice, salt, pepper, and herbs.
4. Mix quinoa with vegetables. Add dressing and toss.
5. Fold in feta gently
6. Gently fold in the crumbled feta cheese, careful not to mash it into the salad.
    Per serving: Calories: 320 kcal, Protein: 9 g, Carbohydrates: 35 g, Fat: 16 g, Fiber: 5 g, Cholesterol: 15 mg, Sodium: 300 mg, Potassium: 450 mg

GREEK SALAD

Servings: 4 servings, Prep Time: 15 minutes, Cook Time: 0 minutes

2 large ripe tomatoes
1 cucumber
1 red onion
1/2 cup Kalamata olives
200 grams (7 oz) feta cheese

3 tablespoons olive oil
1 lemon, juiced
1 teaspoon dried oregano
Salt and freshly ground
black pepper to taste

1. Combine tomatoes, cucumber, and red onion in a large salad bowl.
2. Incorporate olives and feta into the bowl.
3. Whisk olive oil, lemon juice, oregano, salt, and pepper.
4. Drizzle dressing over the salad, toss gently, and garnish with capers and herbs.
    Per serving: Calories: 250 kcal, Protein: 7 g, Carbohydrates: 10 g, Fat: 21 g, Fiber: 2 g, Cholesterol: 25 mg, Sodium: 580 mg, Potassium: 300 mg

TABBOULEH

Servings: 6 servings, Prep Time: 20 minutes (plus time for bulgur to soak), Cook Time: 0 minutes

1 cup bulgur wheat
2 cups boiling water
3 cups fresh parsley
1 cup fresh mint leaves
4 medium tomatoes

4 green onions
1/4 cup extra virgin olive oil
1/4 cup fresh lemon juice
Salt and pepper to taste

1. Place bulgur in a bowl, cover with boiling water, and let soak until water is absorbed and bulgur is tender, about 30 minutes—fluff with a fork and cool.
2. Finely chop parsley, mint, tomatoes, and slice green onions while bulgur soaks.
3. Mix cooled bulgur, parsley, mint, tomatoes, and onions in a large bowl.
4. Whisk olive oil, lemon juice, salt, pepper, and optional spices. Pour over salad and toss.
5. Refrigerate for at least one hour to blend flavors.
    Per serving: Calories: 180 kcal, Protein: 4 g, Carbohydrates: 27 g, Fat: 7g, Fiber: 6 g, Cholesterol: 0 mg, Sodium: 30 mg, Potassium: 450 mg

FATTOUSH

Servings: 4 servings, Prep Time: 20 minutes, Cook Time: 10 minutes (for toasting pita)

2 large pitas
3 tablespoons olive oil
Juice of 1 large lemon
2 garlic cloves
1 teaspoon sumac
Salt and black pepper
1 large cucumber

3 medium tomatoes
4 radishes
2 green onions
1 cup fresh parsley
1/2 cup fresh mint leaves
1 small head romaine lettuce

1. Preheat the oven to 375°F (190°C). Toss the pita squares with 1 tbsp olive oil and bake on a sheet until golden, about 10 minutes. Cool.
2. Whisk lemon juice, 2 tablespoons olive oil, garlic, sumac, salt, and pepper.
3. In a large bowl, mix cucumber, tomatoes, radishes, green onions, parsley, mint, and lettuce
4. Add pita to salad, drizzle with dressing, and toss.
5. Sprinkle with sumac and optional pomegranate seeds
   Per serving: Calories: 230 kcal, Protein: 5 g, Carbohydrates: 27 g, Fat: 12 g, Fiber: 5 g, Cholesterol: 0 mg, Sodium: 300 mg, Potassium: 600 mg

ROASTED BEET AND WALNUT

Servings: 4 servings, Prep Time: 15 minutes, Cook Time: 45 minutes

4 medium beets
1/2 cup walnuts
3 tablespoons olive oil
2 tablespoons balsamic

vinegar
Salt and black pepper
1/4 cup goat cheese
1/2 cup arugula or green

1. Preheat the oven to 400°F (200°C). Wrap the beets in foil and bake until tender, about 45 minutes. Cool, peel, and slice it into wedges.
2. Toast in a skillet over medium heat until golden, about 5-7 minutes.
3. Whisk 2 tbsp olive oil, vinegar, honey, salt, and pepper.
4. Mix beets, walnuts, and greens. Drizzle with dressing, toss, top with goat cheese and herbs.
   Per serving: Calories: 220 kcal, Protein: 6 g, Carbohydrates: 15 g, Fat: 16 g, Fiber: 4 g, Cholesterol: 5 mg, Sodium: 150 mg, Potassium: 400 mg

QUINOA AND BLACK BEAN SALAD

Servings: 6 servings, Prep Time: 15 minutes, Cook Time: 20 minutes

1 cup quinoa, rinsed
2 cups water
1 can (15 oz) black beans
1 large red bell pepper
1/2 red onion
1 cup fresh corn kernels

1/2 cup chopped cilantro
1/4 cup olive oil
Juice of 2 limes
1 teaspoon ground cumin
1/2 teaspoon chili powder
Salt and black pepper

1. In a saucepan, bring quinoa and water to a boil. Reduce heat, cover, and simmer until water is absorbed, about 15 minutes.
2. Combine black beans, bell pepper, onion, and corn in a large salad bowl.
3. Whisk olive oil, lime juice, cumin, chili powder, salt, and pepper.
4. Mix quinoa with salad ingredients. Add dressing and toss. Stir in cilantro.
5. Refrigerate for 30 minutes to blend flavors. Serve chilled or at room temperature.
   Per serving: Calories: 280 kcal, Protein: 9 g, Carbohydrates: 38 g, Fat: 12 g, Fiber: 9 g Cholesterol: 0 mg, Sodium: 200mg, Potassium: 600 mg

SPINACH AND ORZO SALAD

Servings: 4 servings, Prep Time: 10 minutes, Cook Time: 10 minutes

1 cup orzo pasta
2 cups fresh spinach leaves
1/2 cup cherry tomatoes
1/4 cup Kalamata olives
1/4 red onion
1/2 cup feta cheese

For the Dressing:
3 tablespoons olive oil
Juice of 1 lemon
1 garlic clove, minced
1 teaspoon dried oregano
Salt and black pepper

1. Boil orzo in salted water until al dente, about 7-8 minutes.
2. While orzo cooks, prepare vegetables and toast pine nuts if using.
3. Whisk olive oil, lemon juice, garlic, oregano, salt, and pepper.
4. Mix orzo, spinach, tomatoes, olives, onion, feta, and pine nuts in a bowl. Add dressing and toss. Chill: Refrigerate for 30 minutes. Garnish with fresh herbs before serving.
   Per serving: *Calories: 320 kcal, Protein: 10 g, Carbohydrates: 35 g, Fat: 16 g, Fiber: 3 g.*

FRESH CUCUMBER SALAD

Servings:4, Prep Time: 15 minutes, Cooking Time: 0 minutes, Total Time: 15 minutes

2 large cucumbers
1/4 red onion
10 cherry tomatoes
1/4 cup Kalamata olives
1/4 cup feta cheese

2 tablespoons olive oil
Juice of 1 lemon
2 tablespoons fresh dill
Salt and pepper, to taste

1. Combine the sliced cucumbers, red onion, cherry tomatoes, and olives.
2. Sprinkle with chopped dill, dried oregano (if using), salt, and pepper.
3. Drizzle with olive oil and lemon juice. Toss gently to coat all the ingredients evenly.
4. Sprinkle feta cheese over the salad just before serving to maintain its texture.
5. Mix gently once more and serve immediately, or chill in the refrigerator for about 30 minutes.

Per serving: Calories: 140 kcal, Protein: 3 g, Carbohydrates: 8 g, Fats: 11 g, Fiber: 2 g, Cholesterol: 8 mg, Sodium: 200 mg, Potassium: 250 mg

TUNA SALAD

Servings: 4 servings, Prep Time: 15 minutes, Cook Time: 0 minutes

2 cans (each 5 oz) tuna
1 cup cherry tomatoes
1 cucumber
1/2 red bell pepper
1/4 cup red onion
1/4 cup Kalamata olives
1/4 cup feta cheese
2 tablespoons capers

For the Dressing:
3 tablespoons extra virgin olive oil
Juice of 1 lemon
1 garlic clove, minced
1 teaspoon dried oregano
Salt and black pepper

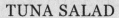

1. Mix tuna, tomatoes, cucumber, bell pepper, onion, olives, and capers in a bowl.
2. Whisk olive oil, lemon juice, garlic, oregano, salt, and pepper.
3. Pour dressing over tuna mixture and toss gently. Sprinkle with feta. Add fresh herbs if desired. Serve immediately or chill for 30 minutes to enhance flavors.

Per serving: Calories: 250 kcal, Protein: 18 g, Carbohydrates: 8 g, Fat: 17 g, Fiber: 2 g, Cholesterol: 30 mg, Sodium: 400 mg, Potassium: 350 mg.

MEDITERRANEAN TOMATO AND MOZZARELLA CAPRESE

Servings: 4 servings, Prep Time: 10 minutes, Cook Time: 0 minutes

4 large ripe tomatoes
8 oz fresh mozzarella cheese
1/4 cup fresh basil leaves
3 tablespoons olive oil

Salt and black pepper
Optional: Crushed red
pepper flakes or fresh
oregano

1. On a platter, alternate and overlap slices of tomato, mozzarella, and basil leaves.
2. Drizzle with olive oil and balsamic vinegar (if using), and season with salt, pepper, and optional red pepper flakes.
3. Enjoy immediately, ideally with crusty bread.
   Per serving: Calories: 290 kcal, Protein: 14 g, Carbohydrates: 6 g, Fat: 24 g, Fiber: 1 g, Cholesterol: 45 mg, Sodium: 280 mg, Potassium: 290 mg

CABBAGE AND CARROT SALAD

Servings: 6 servings, Preparation Time: 15 minutes, Cooking Time: 0 minutes, Total Time: 15 minutes

3 cups green cabbage
2 cups red cabbage
2 large carrots
1/4 cup red onion
1/4 cup fresh parsley
For the Dressing:
3 tablespoons olive oil

2 tablespoons apple cider
vinegar
Juice of 1 lemon
1 teaspoon honey
1 clove garlic, minced
Salt and pepper

1. Combine the green cabbage, red cabbage, carrots, and red onion in a large mixing bowl.
2. In a small bowl, whisk together the olive oil, apple cider vinegar, lemon juice, honey, minced garlic, salt, and pepper until well combined.
3. Pour the dressing over the vegetables in the bowl. Add the chopped parsley and mint if using. Toss everything together until well coated with the dressing.
4. Allow the salad to chill in the refrigerator for at least 30 minutes before serving. This helps the flavors meld together.
   Per serving: Calories: 110 kcal, Protein: 1 g, Carbohydrates: 9 g, Fats: 7 g, Fiber: 2 g, Cholesterol: 0 mg, Sodium: 50 mg

PASTA WITH VEGETABLES

Servings: 6, Preparation Time: 20 minutes, Cooking Time: 10 minutes, Total Time: 30 minutes

12 oz whole-grain
1 cup cherry tomatoes
1 red bell pepper
1 yellow bell pepper
1 cucumber
1/2 red onion
1/4 cup Kalamata olives
1/4 cup feta cheese
1/4 cup fresh basil leaves

2 tablespoons parsley
Dressing:
1/3 cup extra olive oil
3 tablespoons red wine
vinegar
Juice of 1 lemon
2 cloves garlic, minced
1 teaspoon dried oregano
Salt and pepper

1. Cook the pasta according to package instructions.
2. While the pasta cooks, prepare the tomatoes, bell peppers, cucumber, and red onion.
3. Whisk the olive oil, red wine vinegar, lemon juice, minced garlic, oregano, salt, and pepper.
4. Combine the cooled pasta, prepared vegetables, olives, feta cheese, basil, and parsley. bowl.
5. Pour the dressing over the salad and toss to coat evenly.
6. Refrigerate the salad for at least 30 minutes before serving to allow the flavors to meld.
   Per serving: Calories: 320 kcal, Protein: 10 g, Carbohydrates: 45 g, Fats: 12 g, Fiber: 6 g, Cholesterol: 8 mg, Sodium: 180 mg, Potassium: 350 mg

SPRING MILLET PRIMAVERA SALAD

Servings: 4, Preparation Time: 15 minutes, Cooking Time: 25 minutes, Total Time: 40 minutes

1 cup millet
2 cups vegetable broth
1 tablespoon olive oil
2 cloves garlic
1 small zucchini
1 small yellow squash
1/2 cup asparagus
1/2 cup peas

1 carrot
1/2 red bell pepper
1/4 cup fresh basil leaves
1 tablespoon fresh
parsley
Juice of 1 lemon
Salt and pepper
1/4 cup parmesan cheese

1. In a pan, bring the vegetable broth to a boil. Add the millet and simmer it for 20 minutes.
2. Heat olive oil in a large skillet. Add garlic and sauté for 1 minute. Add zucchini, yellow squash, asparagus, peas, carrot, and red bell pepper. Cook for about 5-7 minutes.
3. Add millet to the skillet with the vegetables. Mix gently to combine. Stir in the fresh basil, parsley, and lemon juice.
   Per serving: Calories: 280 kcal, Protein: 8 g, Carbohydrates: 45 g, Fats: 7 g, Fiber: 6 g, Cholesterol: 4 mg, Sodium: 300 mg.

ROASTED BUTTERNUT SQUASH SOUP

Servings: 6, Prep Time: 20 minutes, Cook Time: 50 minutes

1 large butternut squash
3 tablespoons olive oil
Salt and black pepper
1 medium onion
2 carrots
3 cloves garlic

1 teaspoon ground cinnamon
1/2 teaspoon ground nutmeg
4 cups vegetable broth
1 cup water

1. Preheat oven to 400°F (200°C). Toss squash with 2 tbsp olive oil, salt, and pepper. Spread on a baking sheet; add herbs if using. Roast for 30 minutes until golden and soft.
2. Heat the remaining olive oil in a pot. Sauté the onion and carrots for 8 minutes; add garlic, cinnamon, and nutmeg, and cook for 2 more minutes.
3. Add the roasted squash, broth, and water to the pot. Boil and simmer for 20 minutes.
4. Puree with an immersion blender or in batches with a standard blender until smooth.
   Per Serving: Calories: 180, Protein: 2g, Carbs: 30g, Fat: 7g, Fiber: 5g, Sodium: 300mg.

LENTIL SOUP

Servings: 6, Prep Time: 15 minutes, Cook Time: 45 minutes

1 cup dried green lentils
12 tablespoons olive oil
1 large onion
2 carrots
2 celery stalks
3 cloves garlic
1 teaspoon ground cumin

1/2 teaspoon coriander
6 cups vegetable broth
1 can (14.5 oz) tomatoes
Salt and black pepper
2 bay leaves
1 tablespoon lemon juice
1/4 cup fresh parsley

1. Boil vegetable broth in a large pot. Add lentils and bay leaves. Simmer covered until lentils are tender, about 25-30 minutes.
2. Heat olive oil in a skillet over medium. Sauté onion, carrots, and celery until soft, about 5-7 minutes. Add garlic, cumin, coriander, and paprika; cook 2 more minutes.
3. Mix sautéed vegetables and diced tomatoes into the lentils. Season with salt and pepper.
4. Continue simmering for 15 minutes. Remove bay leaves.
5. Stir in lemon juice and parsley or cilantro before serving with whole-grain bread.
   Per serving: Calories: 250 kcal, Protein: 12 g, Carbohydrates: 38 g, Fat: 5 g, Fiber: 15 g, Cholesterol: 0 mg, Sodium: 300 mg, Potassium: 600 mg

FISH SOUP WITH SAFFRON

Servings: 4, Prep Time: 15 minutes, Cook Time: 30 minutes

1 tablespoon olive oil

1 onion

2 cloves garlic

1 fennel bulb

1 carrot

1 pinch saffron threads

4 cups fish stock

1 pound firm white fish

1/2 teaspoon sea salt

1/4 teaspoon black pepper

1/2 cup diced tomatoes

Juice of 1 lemon

2 tablespoons fresh parsley

1. Heat olive oil in a pot over medium heat. Add onion, garlic, fennel, and carrot. Cook until softened, about 5-7 minutes.
2. Stir in saffron, fish stock, and wine. Bring to a simmer.
3. Let the soup simmer for 15 minutes, a step essential for the flavors to meld and develop. If desired, you can also add a bay leaf for an extra layer of aroma.
4. Season fish with salt and pepper, add to pot, and cook until opaque, about 5-10 minutes.
5. Add diced tomatoes and lemon juice and adjust the seasoning. Garnish with parsley.

Per serving: Calories: 230 kcal, Protein: 24 g, Carbohydrates: 10 g, Fat: 8 g, Fiber: 2 g, Cholesterol: 50 mg, Sodium: 600 mg, Potassium: 700 mg.

TOMATO AND BASIL SOUP

Servings: 4, Prep Time: 15 minutes, Cook Time: 30 minutes

2 tablespoons olive oil

1 onion

2 cloves garlic

1 carrot

4 cups fresh ripe tomatoes

1/4 cup fresh basil leaves

3 cups vegetable broth

Salt and black pepper

1. Heat oil in a large pot over medium heat. Sauté onion and garlic until translucent, about 5 minutes. Add carrot and cook for 5 more minutes. It's that simple!
2. Add tomatoes and basil. Cook briefly, then add broth. Bring to a boil, then simmer for 20 minutes.
3. DoN't worry about the blending. You can use an immersion blender or transfer the soup to a blender in batches.
4. Return soup to pot and season with salt and pepper.

Per serving: Calories: 140 kcal, Protein: 3 g, Carbohydrates: 18 g, Fat: 7 g, Fiber: 4 g, Cholesterol: 0 mg, Sodium: 480 mg, Potassium: 650 mg.

GAZPACHO

Servings: 6, Prep Time: 15 minutes, Chill Time: 2 hours, Total Time: 2 hours 15 minutes

6 ripe tomatoes
1 cucumber
1 bell pepper
1 small red onion
2 cloves garlic
2 cups tomato juice

1/4 cup white wine vinegar
1/4 cup olive oil
1/2 tsp sea salt
1/4 tsp black pepper

1. Blend tomatoes, cucumber, bell pepper, onion, and garlic until smooth.
2. Mix in tomato juice, vinegar, olive oil, salt, pepper, and optional spices until well combined.
3. Pour gazpacho into a container, cover, and refrigerate for at least 2 hours to meld flavors.
4. Stir well, adjust seasonings if necessary, and serve chilled with preferred garnishes.
   Per serving: Calories: 150 kcal, Protein: 2 g, Carbohydrates: 15 g, Fat: 10 g, Fiber: 3 g.

AVGOLEMONO

Servings: 4, Prep Time: 10 minutes, Cook Time: 30 minutes, Total Time: 40 minutes

4 cups low-sodium chicken broth
1/2 cup whole-grain rice or orzo
2 large eggs
Juice of 2 lemons
Salt and pepper, to taste
Fresh dill or parsley, chopped

1. In a saucepan, bring chicken broth to a boil. Add rice and simmer until tender, about 20 minutes.
2. Whisk eggs until frothy in a bowl. Gradually add lemon juice. Temper the eggs by slowly whisking a cup of hot broth from the saucepan.
3. Lower the heat to simmer and slowly stir the egg-lemon mixture into the saucepan. Stir continuously until the soup thickens slightly, but do not boil.
4. Season with salt and pepper. Serve garnished with dill or parsley.
   Per serving: Calories: 150 kcal, Protein: 10 g, Carbohydrates: 20 g, Fat: 3 g, Fiber: 1 g

RIBOLLITA

Servings: 6, Prep Time: 20 minutes, Cook Time: 1 hour 30 minutes, Total Time: 1 hour 50 minutes

2 tbsp olive oil

1 onion

2 carrots

2 celery stalks

4 cloves garlic

1 zucchini

1/2 small cabbage

1 bunch swiss chard

1 can (14.5 oz) tomatoes

1 can cannellini beans

6 cups vegetable broth

4 cups day-old whole-grain bread

1/4 cup fresh basil

Salt, black, and red pepper

1. Heat olive oil in a large pot. Add onion, carrots, celery, and garlic, sprinkle with salt, black pepper, and crushed red pepper.
2. Stir in zucchini, cabbage, and swiss chard, cooking until tender.
3. Mix in tomatoes, beans, and broth. Bring to a boil, then simmer partially covered for 1 hour.
4. Add bread pieces and stir into the soup. Simmer until the bread is soaked, about 20 minutes.
5. After heating, stir in fresh basil. Let stand for 10 minutes. Ladle into bowls and top with more basil and grated Parmesan if desired.

Per serving: Calories: 250 kcal, Protein: 8 g, Carbs: 40 g, Fat: 7 g, Fiber: 8 g

MINESTRONE

Servings: 8, Prep Time: 15 minutes, Cook Time: 40 minutes, Total Time: 55 minutes

2 tbsp olive oil

1 large onion

2 carrots

2 celery stalks

4 cloves garlic

1 zucchini

1 yellow squash

1 bell pepper

1 cup green beans

1 (28 oz) tomatoes

6 cups vegetable broth

1 can of kidney beans

1 can cannellini beans

1/2 cup whole wheat pasta or rice

1 tsp dried oregano

1 tsp dried basil

Salt and pepper, to taste

1/4 cup fresh parsley

1. Heat olive oil in a pot. Add onion, carrots, and celery. Cook for 5 minutes. Add garlic, zucchini, squash, bell pepper, and green beans. Cook for 5 more minutes.
2. Pour in tomatoes and broth. Bring to a boil.
3. Stir in kidney beans, cannellini beans, oregano, and basil. Simmer for 20 minutes.
4. Add pasta or rice and cook until tender, about 10-15 minutes.
5. Stir in parsley. Serve hot, topped with optional Parmesan.

Per serving: Calories: 210 kcal, Protein: 9 g, Carbohydrates: 35 g, Fat: 4 g, Fiber: 8 g

LAMB KOFTA

Servings: 4 servings (2 skewers per serving), Prep Time: 30 minutes, Cook Time: 10 minutes

1 pound ground lamb
1 small onion
3 cloves garlic
1/4 cup fresh parsley
2 teaspoons cumin
1 teaspoon coriander

1/2 teaspoon cinnamon
1/4 teaspoon allspice
1/4 teaspoon cayenne pepper
Salt and black pepper
Avocado oil for grilling

1. Mix lamb, onion, garlic, parsley, cilantro, cumin, coriander, cinnamon, allspice, cayenne. Season with salt and pepper. Marinate in the fridge for 20 minutes.
2. Divide the mixture into 8 portions. With moist hands, form each around a skewer into a sausage shape.
3. Heat grill to medium-high and brush with olive oil
4. Grill skewers for about 10 minutes, turning occasionally, until browned and cooked.
   Per serving: Calories: 350 kcal, Protein: 24 g, Carbohydrates: 5 g, Fat: 26 g, Fiber: 1 g, Cholesterol: 85 mg, Sodium: 75 mg, Potassium: 330 mg

HOMEMADE CHORIZO

Servings: 10, Prep Time: 20 minutes, Cook Time: 20 minutes, Total Time: 40 minutes

2 pounds of ground pork
4 cloves garlic
2 tablespoons smoked paprika
1 tablespoon sweet paprika
2 teaspoons ground cumin

1 teaspoon dried oregano
1 teaspoon salt and pepper
1/4 teaspoon cayenne
1 1tablespoon red wine vinegar

1. Combine all ingredients in a large bowl. Mix well to distribute the spices evenly.
2. You can stuff the mixture into casings, twist it into sausages, form it into small patties, or leave it loose. Get creative and let your inspiration guide you.
3. Cook in a skillet over medium heat for about 10 minutes, breaking apart if loose, until browned and cooked. For Sausages: Grill or cook in a skillet for 15-20 minutes, turning occasionally, until evenly browned and cooked.
   Per serving: Calories: 250 kcal, Protein: 22 g, Carbohydrates: 1 g, Fat: 18 g Fiber: 0.5 g, Cholesterol: 70 mg, Sodium: 300 mg, Potassium: 300 mg

ARNI PSITO (SIMPLE GREEK ROAST LAMB)

Servings: 6, Prep Time: 15 minutes, Cook Time: 1 hour 30 minutes, Total Time: 1 hour 45 minutes

3 pounds leg of lamb
4 cloves garlic
1/4 cup olive oil
Juice of 2 lemons
2 teaspoons oregano

1 teaspoon rosemary
1 teaspoon thyme
Salt and black pepper
2 cups water

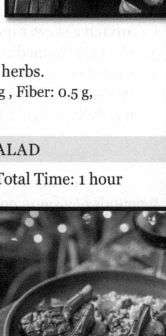

1. Preheat the oven to 350°F (175°C). Cut the lamb into slices and insert the garlic slices.
2. Combine olive oil, lemon juice, oregano, rosemary, thyme, salt, and pepper. Rub over lamb. Marinate for 30 minutes overnight.
3. Place lamb in a roasting pan. Add water or broth. Roast for 1.5 hours or until internal temperature reaches 145°F (63°C) for medium-rare, basting occasionally.
4. Let lamb rest for 15 minutes before carving. Serve with optional fresh herbs.
   Per serving: Calories: 350 kcal, Protein: 25 g, Carbohydrates: 3 g, Fat: 26 g , Fiber: 0.5 g, Cholesterol: 90 mg, Sodium: 120 mg, Potassium: 310 mg

LAMB WITH ROSEMARY AND BULGUR WHEAT SALAD

Servings: 4 servings, Prep Time: 20 minutes, Cook Time: 40 minutes, Total Time: 1 hour

<u>For the Lamb:</u>
4 lamb chops
2 tablespoons olive oil
4 cloves garlic
2 tablespoons rosemary
Salt and black pepper
<u>For the Bulgur Wheat Salad:</u>
1 cup bulgur wheat

2 cups water
1 cucumber, diced
1 large tomato, diced
1/4 cup red onion, finely chopped
1/4 cup parsley
Juice of 1 lemon
3 tablespoons olive oil

1. Mix olive oil, garlic, rosemary, salt, and pepper. Rub over lamb chops and marinate in the fridge for 15 minutes to 1 hour.
2. Boil water, add bulgur and a pinch of salt, reduce heat, cover, and simmer for 12-15 minutes. Let it sit covered for 5 minutes.
3. Grill the lamb chops for 4-5 minutes per side or to your desired doneness.
4. Combine bulgur, cucumber, tomato, onion, and parsley.
   Per serving: Calories: 560 kcal, Protein: 34 g, Carbohydrates: 40 g, Fat: 30 g, Fiber: 9 g, Cholesterol: 90 mg, Sodium: 200 mg, Potassium: 650 mg

GREEK PORK SOUVLAKI

Servings: 4, Prep Time: 15 minutes (plus marinating time), Cook Time: 10 minutes, Total Time: 25

For the Pork Marinade:
1.5 pounds pork tenderloin
3 tablespoons olive oil
Juice of 2 lemons
4 cloves garlic, minced
2 teaspoons dried oregano
1 teaspoon dried thyme
Salt and black pepper
For Serving: Pita bread, Tzatziki sauce, sliced tomatoes, sliced onions

1. In a bowl, combine olive oil, lemon juice, garlic, oregano, thyme, salt, and pepper. Add pork and toss to coat. Cover and refrigerate for at least 2 hours, ideally overnight.
2. Preheat grill to medium-high. Soak wooden skewers in water for 30 minutes if using.
3. Thread marinated pork onto skewers evenly.
4. Grill skewers for about 10 minutes, turning occasionally, until pork is cooked and has char marks.

Per serving: Calories: 310 kcal, Protein: 34 g, Carbohydrates: 3 g, Fat: 18 g, Fiber: 1 g, Cholesterol: 90 mg, Sodium: 150 mg, Potassium: 600 mg

PORCHETTA

Servings: 8, Prep Time: 30 minutes, Cook Time: 2 hours 30 minutes, Total Time: 3 hours

3 pounds pork loin
2 pounds of pork belly
4 cloves garlic
2 tablespoons rosemary
2 tablespoons fennel fronds
1 tablespoon fennel seeds
1 tablespoon fresh sage
Zest of 1 lemon
2 teaspoons sea salt
1 teaspoon black pepper
Olive oil for drizzling

1. Butterfly pork loin if it is thick. Lay pork belly flat.
2. Combine garlic, rosemary, fennel fronds, seeds, sage, lemon zest, salt, and pepper. Rub inside the pork belly and on the loin. Place loin on the belly, roll up, seam down, and tie every 2 inches.
3. Cover and refrigerate overnight to meld flavors.
4. Preheat the oven to 450°F (230°C). Roast on a rack in a roasting pan for 30 minutes, reduce to 325°F (165°C), and roast for 2 more hours. For crispier skin, increase the temperature to 500°F (260°C) for a few minutes at the end.

Per serving: Calories: 580 kcal, Protein: 38 g, Carbohydrates: 1 g, Fat: 47 g, Fiber: 0.5 g, Cholesterol: 135 mg, Sodium: 650 mg, Potassium: 490 mg

DUCK BREAST WITH ORANGE AND POMEGRANATE SAUCE

Servings: 4, Prep Time: 30 minutes, Cook Time: 45 minutes, Total Time: 1 hour 15 minutes

4 duck breasts
Salt and black pepper
2 oranges, zest and juice
1 cup pomegranate juice

1 tablespoon honey
1 teaspoon cornstarch
1 tablespoon thyme

1. Season duck breasts with salt and pepper. Cook skin-side down in a hot skillet over medium heat until fat renders and skin is crisp, about 5-7 minutes. Flip and cook to desired doneness, about five more minutes for medium-rare. Rest before slicing.
2. Drain excess fat in the same pan. Add orange and pomegranate juices, honey, and vinegar. Simmer until reduced by half.
   Per serving: Calories: 800 kcal, Protein: 50 g, Carbohydrates: 70 g, Fat: 35 g, Fiber: 5 g, Cholesterol: 180 mg, Sodium: 300 mg.

TURKEY MEATBALLS IN TOMATO SAUCE

Servings: 4, Prep Time: 15 minutes, Cook Time: 30 minutes, Total Time: 45 minutes

For the Turkey
Meatballs
1 lb ground turkey breast
1/4 cup whole wheat breadcrumbs
1/4 cup parmesan cheese
1 large egg
2 cloves garlic, minced
2 tbsp fresh parsley
1/2 tsp salt

1/4 tsp black pepper
1 tbsp olive oil
For the Tomato Sauce:
2 cups canned tomatoes
1 onion, finely chopped
2 cloves garlic, minced
1 tsp dried oregano
1/2 tsp dried basil
Salt and pepper to taste
1 tbsp olive oil

1. Mix a bowl of turkey, breadcrumbs, Parmesan, egg, garlic, parsley, salt, and pepper. Form into 1-inch balls. Heat olive oil in a skillet. Brown meatballs on all sides for about 10 minutes.
2. In the same skillet, sauté onion and garlic in olive oil until soft. Add tomatoes, oregano, basil, salt, and pepper. Simmer. Return meatballs to skillet, cover, and simmer for 20 minutes.
   Per serving: Calories: 420 kcal, Protein: 36 g, Carbohydrates: 47 g, Fat: 12 g, Fiber: 5 g, Cholesterol: 98 mg, Sodium: 700 mg, Potassium: 670 mg

CHICKEN PIRI PIRI

Servings: 4, Prep Time: 15 minutes (plus marinating), Cook Time: 30 minutes, Total Time: 45 minutes

4 chicken breasts
3 tbsp olive oil
4 cloves garlic
2 red chili peppers
Juice of 2 lemons
1 tbsp paprika
1 tsp dried oregano

Salt and black pepper
For Serving:
Lemon wedges
Fresh parsley, chopped
Mixed greens salad or
grilled vegetable

1. Blend olive oil, garlic, chili peppers, lemon juice, paprika, smoked paprika, oregano, cayenne, salt, and pepper until smooth.
2. Coat chicken breasts in the marinade. Refrigerate for at least 2 hours, ideally overnight.
3. Preheat the grill to medium-high. Grill the marinated chicken for 6-7 minutes per side until the internal temperature is 165°F (74°C). Rest the chicken briefly after grilling, then slice. Garnish with parsley and lemon wedges.

Per serving: Calories: 290 kcal, Protein: 35 g, Carbohydrates: 3 g, Fats: 15 g, Fiber: 1 g, Cholesterol: 85 mg, Sodium: 200 mg, Potassium: 500 m

PECAN-CRUSTED TURKEY CUTLETS

Servings: 4, Prep Time: 15 minutes, Cook Time: 10 minutes, Total Time: 25 minutes

4 turkey breast cutlets
1 cup finely chopped pecans
1/2 cup all-purpose flour
2 large eggs
1 tbsp water

1 tsp paprika
Salt and pepper
2 tbsp olive oil
Lemon wedges for serving

1. Season turkey cutlets with salt, pepper, and paprika.
2. Set three plates for dredging: one with flour, one with beaten eggs mixed with water, and one with chopped pecans.
3. Coat each cutlet in flour, dip in egg mixture, then press into pecans.
4. Heat olive oil in a skillet over medium-high. Fry cutlets for 4-5 minutes per side until golden and cooked through.
5. Serve hot with lemon wedges.

Per serving: Calories: 390, Protein: 27g, Carbohydrates: 9g, Fat: 29g, Fiber: 2g.

QUICK CATALAN CHICKEN

Servings: 4, Prep: 20 minutes, Cook: 1 hour, Total: 1 hour 20 minutes

4 chicken thighs
4 chicken drumsticks
Salt and black pepper
2 tbsp olive oil
1 large onion, sliced
4 cloves garlic
1 cup chicken broth

1/2 cup prunes
1/2 cup green olives
1/4 cup pine nuts
2 tsp fresh thyme
1 tsp fresh rosemary
1 bay leaf

1. Preheat the oven to 375°F (190°C).
2. Season the chicken with salt and pepper.
3. Brown the chicken in olive oil over medium-high heat until golden, about 5-7 minutes per side, then set aside.
4. Sauté onion until soft. Add garlic and cook for another minute.
5. Add broth, prunes, olives, pine nuts, thyme, rosemary, and bay leaf. Stir to combine.
6. Return chicken to skillet, cover with sauce, and bake uncovered for 45 minutes.
    Per serving: Calories: 560 kcal, Protein: 38 g, Carbohydrates: 23 g, Fat: 32 g, Fiber: 3 g, Cholesterol: 190 mg, Sodium: 400 mg, Potassium: 600 mg

CABBAGE ROLLS WITH LAMB AND RICE

Servings: 6, Prep Time: 30 minutes, Cook Time: 1 hour 30 minutes, Total Time: 2 hours

12 cabbage leaves
1 lb ground lamb
1 cup cooked rice
1 chopped onion
2 cloves garlic
1 beaten egg
2 tbsp chopped parsley
1 tsp dried mint

Salt and pepper to taste
For the Sauce:
1 can (28 oz) tomatoes
2 tbsp tomato paste
1 cup water
2 cloves garlic, minced
Salt and pepper to taste

1. Blanch in boiling water for 2-3 minutes. Drain and cool.
2. Mix lamb, rice, onion, garlic, egg, parsley, mint, salt, and pepper.
3. Place filling on each leaf, fold sides, and roll.
4. Combine the tomatoes, tomato paste, water, garlic, sugar, salt, and pepper in a pot and simmer.
5. Add rolls to the sauce, cover, and simmer for 1.5 hours until tender.
6. Plate rolls with sauce and garnish with parsley.
    Per serving: 350 kcal, 22 g protein, 27 g carbohydrates, 18 g fat, 5 g fiber.

BAKED TROUT WITH LEMON AND HERBS

Servings: 4 servings, Prep Time: 10 minutes, Cook Time: 20 minutes, Total Time: 30 minutes

4 trout fillets
2 lemons
4 tablespoons olive oil
4 cloves garlic

2 tablespoons parsley
1 tablespoon fresh dill
1 teaspoon thyme leaves
Salt and black pepper

1. Preheat your oven to 400°F (200°C).
2. Rinse the trout fillets under cold water and pat dry with paper towels. Lay the fillets skin-side down in a baking dish large enough to accommodate them in a single layer.
3. Mix the olive oil, lemon juice, minced garlic, parsley, dill, and thyme. Drizzle the herb mixture over the trout fillets, ensuring they are well coated. Season each fillet with salt and pepper to taste. Arrange lemon slices over the top of the fillets.
4. Place the baking dish in the oven and bake for 15-20 minutes.
   Per serving: Calories: 300 kcal, Protein: 28 g, Carbohydrates: 2 g, Fat: 20 g Fiber: 0.5 g, Cholesterol: 80 mg, Sodium: 75 mg, Potassium: 500 mg

GARLIC BUTTER SHRIMP RECIPE

Servings: 4, Prep Time: 10 minutes, Cook Time: 10 minutes, Total Time: 20 minutes

1 pound large shrimp
4 tablespoons olive oil
3 tablespoons butter
6 cloves garlic

Juice of 1 lemon
2 tablespoons parsley
1/2 teaspoon red pepper
Salt and pepper to taste

1. Rinse the shrimp under cold water and pat dry with paper towels.
2. Heat olive oil and butter over medium heat in a large skillet until the butter is melted. Sauté for 1-2 minutes until the garlic is fragrant but not browned.
3. Increase the heat to medium-high and add the shrimp to the skillet in a single layer. Season with salt and black pepper. Cook for about 2 minutes on one side, then flip and cook for another 1-2 minutes.
4. Squeeze lemon juice over the cooked shrimp and sprinkle with chopped parsley. Toss to combine and coat the shrimp evenly with the sauce.
   Per serving: Calories: 280 kcal, Protein: 24 g, Carbohydrates: 2 g, Fat: 20 g, Fiber: 0 g, Cholesterol: 180 mg, Sodium: 300 mg, Potassium: 200 mg

SEAFOOD PAELLA

Servings: 6, Prep Time: 20 minutes, Cook Time: 40 minutes, Total Time: 1 hour

2 tbsp olive oil
1 large onion
3 cloves garlic
1 red bell pepper
1 yellow bell pepper
1 cup tomatoes
1 tsp smoked paprika
1/2 tsp saffron threads
2 cups short-grain rice

(paella or Arborio)
4 cups vegetable broth
1 lb mixed seafood (shrimp, mussels, clams, cleaned)
1/2 lb squid
1 cup frozen peas
Salt and black pepper
Lemon wedges and fresh parsley for garnish

1. Heat olive oil over medium in a large skillet or paella pan. Cook the onion, garlic, and bell peppers until soft.
2. Add tomatoes, smoked paprika, and saffron to the pan. Stir in rice until coated, then pour in vegetable broth. Simmer for 20 minutes.
3. Place the seafood and squid over the rice. Cover and cook until the shellfish is open and the shrimp are opaque, for about 15 minutes. Mix in the peas during the last 5 minutes.
4. Adjust salt and pepper. Let sit for a few minutes off the heat.
   Per serving: Calories: 450 kcal Protein: 30 g Carbohydrates: 65 g Fat: 8 g Fiber: 4 g Cholesterol: 175 mg Sodium: 300 mg, Calories: 450 kcal, Protein: 30 g, Carbohydrates: 65 g, Fat: 8 g, Fiber: 4 g, Cholesterol: 175 mg, Sodium: 300 mg.

GRILLED OCTOPUS WITH OREGANO AND CHILI

Servings: 4, Prep Time: 30 minutes (plus marinating), Cook Time: 1 hour 20 minutes, Total Time: 1 hour 50 minutes

1 giant octopus
2 tbsp olive oil
2 cloves garlic
1 tsp dried oregano

1 tsp crushed red chili flakes
Juice of 1 lemon
Salt and black pepper
Lemon wedges and parsley

1. Blanch the octopus in boiling water for 2 minutes, then cool.
2. Mix olive oil, garlic, oregano, chili flakes, lemon juice, salt, and pepper. Marinate the octopus for at least 2 hours.
3. Preheat oven to 300°F. Bake the octopus in a covered dish for 1 hour.
4. Grill the octopus over high heat for 3-5 minutes on each side.
   Per serving: Calories: 200 kcal, Protein: 25 g, Carbs: 5 g, Fats: 10 g, Fiber: 1 g, Cholesterol: 75 mg, Sodium: 450 mg

BAKED SARDINES WITH VINE TOMATOES

Servings: 4, Prep Time: 15 minutes, Cook Time: 20 minutes, Total Time: 35 minutes

12 fresh sardines
4 vine tomatoes
4 cloves garlic
2 tbsp olive oil

Juice of 1 lemon
1/2 tsp dried oregano
Salt and black pepper
Fresh parsley

1. Preheat the oven to 375°F (190°C).
2. Rinse and pat dry. Mix olive oil, lemon juice, oregano, chili flakes, salt, and pepper. Brush the mixture over the sardines.
3. Lay sliced tomatoes in a baking dish, top with sardines, and sprinkle with garlic.
4. Bake for 20 minutes or until sardines are cooked through.
5. Garnish with fresh parsley.
   Per serving: Calories: 220 kcal, Protein: 25 g, Carbohydrates: 5 g, Fats: 12 g, Fiber: 1 g, Cholesterol: 85 mg, Sodium: 340 mg

MUSSELS IN WHITE WINE SAUCE WITH BASIL

Servings: 4, Prep Time: 15 minutes, Cook Time: 10 minutes, Total Time: 25 minutes

2 lbs fresh mussels
1 tbsp olive oil
4 cloves garlic
1 shallot
1 cup dry white wine

1 cup vegetable broth
Juice of 1 lemon
1/2 cup fresh basil
Salt and black pepper
Fresh parsley for garnish

1. Rinse under cold water, removing beards. Discard any that don't close when tapped.
2. Heat olive oil in a large pot. Sauté garlic and shallot until soft, about 2-3 minutes.
3. Add white wine, vegetable broth, and lemon juice to the pot; bring to a simmer. Add mussels, cover, and cook for about 5-7 minutes. Discard any that remain closed.
4. Stir in chopped basil and season with salt, pepper, and red pepper flakes.
   Per serving: Calories: 250 kcal, Protein: 20 g, Carbohydrates: 8 g, Fat: 8 g, Cholesterol: 50 mg, Sodium: 300 mg

GRILLED MACKEREL

Servings: 4 servings, Prep Time: 15 minutes, Cook Time: 10 minutes, Total Time: 25 minutes

4 whole mackerel

4 tablespoons olive oil

2 lemons

4 cloves garlic

2 tablespoons fresh parsley

1 teaspoon dried oregano

Salt and black pepper

1. Rinse the mackerel under cold water and pat dry with paper towels. Make several diagonal slashes on both sides of each fish.
2. In a bowl, mix olive oil, lemon juice, minced garlic, parsley, oregano, salt, and black pepper. Rub this mixture both inside the fish and on the slashes. Place lemon slices inside the cavity of each fish. Let the fish marinate for about 10 minutes.
3. Preheat your grill to medium-high heat.
4. Grill for 5 minutes on each side until the skin is crispy and the flesh flakes easily with a fork.
   Per serving: Calories: 320 kcal, Protein: 23 g, Carbohydrates: 2 g, Fat: 25 g, Fiber: 0.5 g, Cholesterol: 60 mg, Sodium: 120 mg, Potassium: 560 mg

COD EN PAPILLOTE WITH TOMATOES, OLIVES, AND CAPERS

Servings: 4, Prep Time: 15 minutes, Cook Time: 15 minutes, Total Time: 30 minutes

4 cod fillets

2 tablespoons olive oil

1 cup cherry tomatoes

1/2 cup olives

1/4 cup capers

4 cloves garlic

Juice of 1 lemon

4 sprigs fresh thyme

Salt and black pepper 4

large pieces of parchment

paper

1. Preheat your oven to 400°F (200°C).
2. Cut four large squares of parchment paper to envelop each cod.
3. Drizzle each piece of parchment paper with olive oil. Season each fillet with salt and pepper. Top each fillet with cherry tomatoes, olives, capers, and garlic slices. Drizzle lemon juice over each fillet and add a sprig of thyme.
4. Fold the parchment paper over the fish, twisting the ends to seal each packet securely, creating a parcel to steam the fish.
5. Place the packets on a baking sheet and bake in the oven for about 15 minutes, until the fish is cooked and flakes easily with a fork.
   Per serving: Calories: 230 kcal, Protein: 28 g, Carbohydrates: 5 g, Fat: 11 g, Fiber: 1 g, Cholesterol: 60 mg, Sodium: 400 mg, Potassium: 650 mg

BAKED SEA BASS WITH LEMON AND HERBS

Servings: 4, Prep Time: 10 minutes, Cook Time: 20 minutes, Total Time: 30 minutes

4 sea bass fillets)
2 tablespoons olive oil
2 lemons
4 cloves garlic

2 tablespoons parsley
1 tablespoon fresh dill
1 tablespoon fresh basil
Salt black pepper to taste

1. Preheat your oven to 400°F (200°C).
2. Rinse the sea bass fillets under cold water and pat dry with paper towels. Arrange the fillets in a single layer in a baking dish.
3. Drizzle the olive oil and lemon juice over the fillets. Sprinkle with minced garlic, parsley, dill, basil, salt, and pepper.
4. Place a few lemon slices on top of each fillet to add lemon flavor as the fish bakes.
5. Bake in the oven for 15-20 minutes.
   Per serving: Calories: 230 kcal, Protein: 23 g, Carbohydrates: 3 g, Fat: 14 g, Fiber: 1 g, Cholesterol: 60 mg, Sodium: 75 mg, Potassium: 450 mg

GRILLED CALAMARI WITH A SQUEEZE OF LEMON

Servings: 4, Prep Time: 10 minutes, Cook Time: 5 minutes, Total Time: 45 minutes

1 pound whole calamari
3 tablespoons olive oil
2 cloves garlic
Salt and black pepper

2 lemons, one for juice
and one cut into wedges
for serving
Fresh parsley

1. In a large bowl, combine the olive oil, minced garlic, juice of one lemon, salt, black pepper, and red pepper flakes. Add the calamari and toss to coat evenly. Cover and let marinate in the refrigerator for at least 30 minutes.
2. Preheat a grill or grill pan to high heat. Ensure it is hot before adding the calamari to achieve a good sear without overcooking.
3. Remove the calamari from the marinade, letting excess oil drip off to prevent flare-ups. Grill the calamari over high heat for 2-3 minutes on each side or until they are cooked through and have grill marks.
   Per serving: Calories: 180 kcal, Protein: 18 g, Carbohydrates: 5 g, Fat: 10 g, Fiber: 1 g, Cholesterol: 264 mg, Sodium: 90 mg, Potassium: 300 mg

BAKED TROUT WITH WALNUT CRUST

Servings: 4 servings, Prep Time: 15 minutes, Cook Time: 15 minutes, Total Time: 30 minutes

trout fillets
1 cup walnuts
1/4 cup whole wheat
breadcrumbs
2 tablespoons parsley

1 clove garlic
2 tablespoons olive oil
Zest of 1 lemon
Salt and black pepper
Lemon wedges for serving

1. Preheat your oven to 400°F (200°C).
2. Combine the finely chopped walnuts, breadcrumbs, chopped parsley, minced garlic, lemon zest, and 1 tablespoon of olive oil. Mix until well combined and slightly moist.
3. Pat the trout fillets dry with paper towels. Brush them with the remaining tablespoon of olive oil and season both sides.
4. Press the walnut mixture onto the top of each trout fillet, covering the surface.
5. Bake in the oven for 12-15 minutes until the crust is golden.
   Per serving: Calories: 350 kcal, Protein: 28 g, Carbohydrates: 8 g, Fat: 24 g, Fiber: 2 g, Cholesterol: 80 mg, Sodium: 120 mg, Potassium: 560 mg

GRILLED SALMON WITH A SIDE OF ASPARAGUS

Servings: 4, Prep Time: 10 minutes, Cook Time: 15 minutes, Total Time: 25 minutes

For the Grilled Salmon:
4 salmon fillets
2 tablespoons olive oil
Juice of 1 lemon
2 cloves garlic, minced
1 teaspoon dried dill

For the Asparagus:
1 pound asparagus
1 tablespoon olive oil
Salt and black pepper
Lemon wedges for serving

1. Preheat the grill to medium-high heat. Ensure the grates are clean to prevent sticking.
2. Whisk together olive oil, lemon juice, minced garlic, dill, salt, and black pepper. Brush the salmon fillets with the marinade and let them marinate for 10 minutes.
3. Toss the trimmed asparagus with olive oil, salt, and black pepper in a mixing bowl.
4. Place the asparagus perpendicular to the grates on the preheated grill. Cook for about 7-10 minutes, turning occasionally, until tender and lightly charred.
5. Grill for 5-6 minutes on each side until the salmon is cooked and flakes easily with a fork.
   Per serving: Calories: 360 kcal, Protein: 35 g, Carbohydrates: 5 g, Fat: 22 g, Fiber: 2 g, Cholesterol: 90 mg, Sodium: 200 mg.
6.

SHRIMP SAGANAKI

Servings: 4 servings, Prep Time: 15 minutes, Cook Time: 20 minutes, Total Time: 35 minutes

1 pound large shrimp
2 tablespoons olive oil
1 onion
3 cloves garlic
1/2 cup dry white wine
1 can tomatoes

1 teaspoon dried oregano
1 teaspoon dried basil
salt and black pepper
1 cup feta cheese
1/4 cup fresh parsley
Juice of 1 lemon

1. Rinse the shrimp and pat dry—season lightly with salt and pepper.
2. Heat the olive oil in a large skillet over medium heat. Add the chopped onion and cook until translucent, about 5 minutes. Add the minced garlic and cook for another 1 minute.
3. Pour in the white wine, letting it simmer for about 3-4 minutes.
4. Stir in the diced tomatoes with their juices, oregano, and basil—season with salt and pepper. Simmer the sauce for about 10 minutes until it thickens slightly.
5. Add them to the skillet, nestling them into the sauce. Cook for about 5 minutes.
6. Sprinkle the crumbled feta over the shrimp. Cover and cook for 5 minutes.
7. Squeeze lemon juice over the dish and garnish with chopped parsley.
    Per serving: Calories: 350 kcal, Protein: 25 g, Carbohydrates: 15 g, Fat: 18 g, Fiber: 2 g, Cholesterol: 180 mg, Sodium: 850 mg.

BAKED COD WITH BROCCOLI

Servings: 4, Prep Time: 10 minutes, Cook Time: 20 minutes, Total Time: 30 minutes

4 cod fillets
4 cups broccoli florets
3 tablespoons olive oil
2 cloves garlic, minced
Juice of 1 lemon

1 teaspoon dried thyme
Salt and freshly ground
black pepper
Lemon wedges for
serving

1. Preheat your oven to 400°F (200°C).
2. Toss the broccoli florets with 1 tablespoon of olive oil, salt, and pepper.
3. Mix 2 tablespoons of olive oil, minced garlic, lemon juice, thyme, salt. Place the cod fillets on the other half of the baking sheet. Brush each fillet with the olive oil and lemon mixture. If desired, sprinkle grated parmesan cheese over the fillets for added flavor.
4. Place the baking sheet in the oven and bake for 15-20 minutes.
    Per serving: Calories: 280 kcal, Protein: 28 g, Carbohydrates: 8 g, Fat: 16 g, Fiber: 3 g, Cholesterol: 60 mg, Sodium: 200 mg.

LENTIL AND VEGETABLE STUFFED PEPPERS

Servings: 4, Prep Time: 20 minutes, Cook Time: 40 minutes, Total Time: 60 minutes

4 large bell peppers	1 carrot
1 cup dried lentils	1 cup chopped tomatoes
2 tablespoons olive oil	1 teaspoon oregano
1 onion	1 teaspoon dried basil
2 cloves garlic	Salt and black pepper
1 zucchini	1/4 cup fresh parsley

1. Set to 375°F (190°C). Arrange bell peppers in a baking dish.
2. Cook lentils as per package instructions until tender, then drain.
3. In a skillet, heat olive oil over medium. Sauté onion and garlic until onion is translucent. Add zucchini and carrot; cook until softened, about 5 minutes. Stir in tomatoes, oregano, basil, salt, and pepper. Cook for another 5 minutes.
4. Mix cooked lentils with the sautéed vegetable mixture in a large bowl. Add parsley.
5. Fill each pepper with the lentil mixture and top with feta if using.
6. Cover with foil and bake for 30 minutes. Remove foil; bake for another 10 minutes.
   Per serving: Calories: 320 kcal, Protein: 14 g, Carbohydrates: 45 g, Fat: 10 g, Fiber: 12 g, Cholesterol: 10 mg (if using feta), Sodium: 200 mg, Potassium: 800 mg

BROCCOLI AND FETA OMELET

Servings: 2, Prep Time: 10 minutes, Cook Time: 10 minutes, Total Time: 20 minutes

4 large eggs	1/2 cup feta cheese
2 tablespoons milk	2 tablespoons olive oil
1 cup broccoli florets,	Salt and freshly ground
finely chopped	black pepper

1. In a bowl, beat the eggs with the milk, salt, pepper, and oregano (if using) until well combined. Set aside. Steam the broccoli florets until just tender, about 3-4 minutes, then chop them into small pieces if they aren't already finely chopped.
2. Heat the olive oil in a non-stick skillet over medium heat. Add the chopped broccoli and sauté for about 2 minutes until slightly tender. Pour the egg mixture over the broccoli. Sprinkle the crumbled feta evenly over the top.
3. Cover and cook for 5-7 minutes until the eggs are set and the bottom is golden.
   Per serving: Calories: 350 kcal, Protein: 22 g, Carbohydrates: 5 g, Fat: 27 g, Fiber: 2 g, Cholesterol: 370 mg, Sodium: 550 mg, Potassium: 300 mg

RATATOUILLE WITH WHOLE GRAIN PASTA

Servings: 4, Prep Time: 15 minutes, Cook Time: 45 minutes, Total Time: 1 hour

For the Ratatouille:
1 eggplant
2 zucchinis
1 yellow bell pepper
1 red bell pepper
1 onion
3 cloves garlic
3 tomatoes

1/4 cup olive oil
1 teaspoon dried basil
Salt and black pepper
Fresh basil leaves for garnish
For the Pasta:
8 ounces whole grain pasta

1. Preheat the oven to 375°F (190°C). In a large mixing bowl, toss the eggplant, zucchini, bell peppers, onion, and garlic with olive oil, thyme, basil, salt, and pepper until evenly coated.
2. Spread the vegetables in a single layer on a large baking sheet. Roast in the preheated oven for about 35-40 minutes, stirring halfway through, until vegetables are tender and lightly browned.
3. Bring a large pot of salted water to a boil while the vegetables roast. Cook the whole-grain pasta.
4. Combine the roasted vegetables with the cooked pasta in a large skillet over medium heat.
Per serving: Calories: 400 kcal, Protein: 12 g, Carbohydrates: 60 g, Fat: 14 g, Fiber: 11 g, Cholesterol: 0 mg, Sodium: 200 mg.

VEGETABLE STIR-FRY WITH BROWN RICE

Servings: 4, Prep Time: 15 minutes, Cook Time: 30 minutes, Total Time: 45 minutes

1 tbsp olive oil
1 onion, sliced
2 cloves garlic
1 red bell pepper
1 yellow bell pepper
2 zucchinis
1 carrot
1 cup snap peas

1 cup broccoli florets
2 tbsp soy sauce
1 tbsp balsamic vinegar
1 tsp sesame oil
Salt and pepper
2 tbsp fresh parsle1 cup brown rice
2 cups water

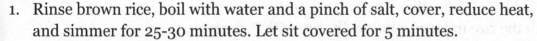

1. Rinse brown rice, boil with water and a pinch of salt, cover, reduce heat, and simmer for 25-30 minutes. Let sit covered for 5 minutes.
2. Heat olive oil in a skillet over medium-high. Sauté onion and garlic until translucent. Add bell peppers, zucchini, carrot, snap peas, and broccoli; stir-fry until crisp-tender. Season with salt in soy sauce, balsamic vinegar, and sesame oil. Cook for 2 more minutes.
Per serving: Calories: 320 kcal, Protein: 8 g, Carbohydrates: 55 g, Fat: 7 g, Fiber: 6 g, Cholesterol: 0 mg, Sodium: 400 mg.

SPAGHETTI WITH MARINARA SAUCE

Servings: 4. Prep Time: 10 minutes, Cook Time: 20 minutes, Total Time: 30 minutes

2 tbsp olive oil
1 onion
3 cloves garlic
28 oz can crush tomatoes
1 tsp dried basil

1 tsp dried oregano
Salt and black pepper
Fresh basil leaves for garnish
12 oz whole grain spaghetti

1. Heat olive oil in a saucepan over medium. Sauté onion until translucent (~5 minutes). Add garlic; cook 1 minute. Stir in tomatoes, basil, oregano, salt, pepper, and red pepper flakes. Simmer on low for 15-20 minutes.
2. Boil spaghetti in salted water until al dente; drain
3. Toss spaghetti with sauce.
   Per serving: Calories: 390 kcal, Protein: 14 g, Carbohydrates: 72 g, Fat: 8 g, Fiber: 10 g, Cholesterol: 0 mg, Sodium: 300 mg.

STUFFED TOMATOES WITH RICE AND HERBS

Servings: 4, Prep Time: 20 minutes, Cook Time: 30 minutes, Total Time: 50 minutes

4 large tomatoes
1 cup cooked brown rice
2 tbsp olive oil
1 onion
2 cloves garlic

1/4 cup fresh parsley
1/4 cup fresh basil
1 tsp dried oregano
Salt and pepper

1. Cut the tops off the tomatoes and scoop out the insides, setting the flesh aside. Place the hollowed tomatoes in a baking dish.
2. Heat olive oil in a skillet. Sauté onion and garlic until translucent. Add chopped tomato flesh, pine nuts, and raisins; cook 5 minutes. Mix in rice, parsley, basil, and oregano—season with salt and pepper. Cook until heated through.
3. Fill tomatoes with the rice mixture. Optionally, top with Parmesan.
4. Preheat the oven to 375°F (190°C). Cover the tomatoes with foil and bake for 20 minutes. Remove the foil and bake for 10 more minutes until tender.
   Per serving: Calories: 230 kcal, Protein: 5 g, Carbohydrates: 28 g, Fat: 12 g, Fiber: 5 g, Cholesterol: 4 mg, Sodium: 150 mg.

SAFFRON RICE

Servings: 4, Cook Time: 20 minutes, Total Time: 25 minutes

1 cup basmati rice
2 cups water
1 tbsp olive oil
1 small onion
Pinch of saffron threads,

soaked in 2 tbsp warm
water
1/4 tsp cardamom powder
Salt, to taste
2 tbsp parsley

1. Rinse basmati rice under cold water until clear. Drain well.
2. Heat olive oil in a saucepan over medium heat. Sauté onion until translucent and slightly golden, about 5 minutes.
3. Add rice, saffron with soaking water, cardamom, and salt to the onions. Stir to combine. Pour in 2 cups of water, bring to a boil, then reduce heat to low. Cover and simmer for 15-20 minutes.
Per serving: Calories: 210 kcal, Protein: 4 g, Carbohydrates: 40 g, Fat: 4 g, Fiber: 1 g, Cholesterol: 0 mg, Sodium: 10 mg.

COUSCOUS WITH VEGETABLES

Servings: 4, Prep Time: 10 minutes, Cook Time: 20 minutes, Total Time: 30 minutes

1 cup whole wheat couscous
1 1/4 cups water
1 tablespoon olive oil
1 onion, diced
2 cloves garlic
1 zucchini, diced
1 bell pepper
1 carrot

1 cup cherry tomatoes
1/2 cup frozen peas
Salt and black pepper
1 teaspoon dried basil
1/2 teaspoon dried thyme
2 tablespoons parsley
Juice of 1 lemon

1. In a saucepan, bring water to a boil. Add the couscous, stir once, and remove from heat. Cover and let stand for 5 minutes.
2. Heat olive oil in a skillet over medium heat. Add the onion and garlic, sautéing about 3-4 minutes. Add the zucchini, bell pepper, and carrot. Cook for about 7-8 minutes. Stir in the cherry tomatoes and peas, cooking about 3 minutes.
3. Add the cooked couscous to the skillet with the vegetables. Stir in dried basil, thyme, and fresh parsley—season with salt and pepper. Drizzle with lemon juice and mix well.
Per serving: Calories: 240 kcal, Protein: 8 g, Carbohydrates: 45 g, Fat: 5 g, Fiber: 7 g, Cholesterol: 0 mg, Sodium: 75 mg, Potassium: 450 mg

EGGPLANT MOUSSAKA

Servings: 6 servings, Prep Time: 30 minutes, Cook Time: 1 hour, Total Time: 1 hour 30 minutes

For the Eggplant:
3 large eggplants
3 tablespoons olive oil
Salt and pepper
1 can tomatoes
1 teaspoon cinnamon
1 teaspoon oregano
Salt and black pepper

For the Béchamel Sauce:
2 cups milk
4 tablespoons unsalted butter
4 tablespoons flour
1/4 teaspoon nutmeg
1/2 cup grated Parmesan

1. Preheat the oven to 400°F (200°C). Brush the eggplant slices with olive oil and season with salt and pepper. Roast for 25-30 minutes, flipping halfway through.
2. Melt butter over medium heat in a saucepan. Whisk in flour and cook for 2 minutes. Gradually add milk, whisking continuously until the sauce thickens. Season with nutmeg, salt, and pepper. Remove from heat and stir in Parmesan cheese.
3. Layer half the roasted eggplant slices in a greased baking dish. Pour the béchamel sauce over the top, smoothing with a spatula.
   Per serving: Calories: 530 kcal, Protein: 25 g, Carbohydrates: 35 g, Fat: 32 g, Fiber: 9 g, Cholesterol: 90 mg, Sodium: 400 mg, Potassium: 900 mg

POTATO VEGETABLE HASH

Servings: 4, Prep Time: 15 minutes, Cook Time: 30 minutes, Total Time: 45 minutes

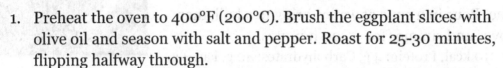

2 tbsp olive oil
4 large potatoes
1 onion
1 red bell pepper
1 green bell pepper
2 cloves garlic

1 zucchini
1 cup cherry tomatoes
1 tsp smoked paprika
1/2 tsp dried thyme
Salt and black pepper
1/4 cup fresh parsley

1. Heat olive oil in a large skillet over medium heat. Add diced potatoes and cook until they soften and turn golden, about 10-15 minutes.
2. Add onion, red and green bell peppers, and garlic to the skillet. Cook for 5 minutes until the onions are translucent. Stir in zucchini and cherry tomatoes. Cook for another 5 minutes.
3. Sprinkle the vegetables with smoked paprika, thyme, salt, and pepper.
   Per serving: Calories: 300 kcal, Protein: 12 g, Carbohydrates: 45 g, Fat: 10 g, Fiber: 6 g, Cholesterol: 0 mg, Sodium: 200 mg, Potassium: 1050 mg

SPICED CHICKPEA WRAP WITH TAHINI SAUCE

Servings: 4, Prep Time: 15 minutes, Cook Time: 10 minutes, Total Time: 25 minutes

1 can (15 oz) chickpeas
1 tbsp olive oil
1 tsp cumin
1 tsp smoked paprika
1/2 tsp garlic powder
Salt and black pepper
1/4 cup tahini
Juice of 1 lemon
2 tbsp water

1 clove garlic
4 whole grain flatbreads
1 cup mixed greens (e.g., spinach, arugula)
1 cucumber
1 carrot
1 red bell pepper
Fresh parsley

1. Heat olive oil in a skillet over medium heat. Add chickpeas, cumin, smoked paprika, garlic powder, salt, and pepper. Cook for 5-7 minutes.
2. In a small bowl, whisk the tahini, lemon juice, water, minced garlic, and salt until creamy.
3. Spread tahini sauce on each flatbread. Layer with mixed greens, cucumber, carrot, and bell pepper. Top with spiced chickpeas and parsley. Roll up tightly.
   Per serving: Calories: 400 kcal, Protein: 15 g, Carbohydrates: 55 g, Fat: 16 g, Fiber: 12 g, Cholesterol: 0 mg, Sodium: 300 mg.

ARTICHOKE AND SPINACH PIZZA ON A WHOLE-GRAIN CRUST

Servings: 4, Prep Time: 20 minutes, Cook Time: 15 minutes, Total Time: 35 minutes

1 cup whole wheat flour
1 cup all-purpose flour
1 packet of instant yeast
3/4 cup warm water
2 tbsp olive oil
1/2 tsp salt
1 tbsp olive oil

2 cloves garlic
2 cups fresh spinach
1 can artichoke hearts
1/2 cup ricotta cheese
1 cup mozzarella cheese
Salt and black
1 tsp dried oregano

1. Combine whole wheat flour, yeast, sugar, and salt in a large bowl. Add warm water and olive oil. Stir until the dough begins to come together. Knead on a floured surface until smooth and elastic, about 5 minutes. Cover and let rise for about 1 hour.
2. Set to 475°F (245°C). Place a pizza stone inside to heat.
3. Heat olive oil in a skillet. Sauté garlic for 30 seconds, then add spinach and cook until wilted.
4. Roll out the dough. Spread ricotta on the crust and top with spinach, artichoke hearts, and mozzarella, and sprinkle with oregano and optional red pepper flakes. Bake for 12-15 minutes.
   Per serving: Calories: 450 kcal, Protein: 20 g, Carbohydrates: 55 g, Fat: 18 g, Fiber: 8 g, Cholesterol: 30 mg, Sodium: 600 mg.

SHAKSHUKA

Servings: 4, Prep Time: 10 minutes, Cook Time: 20 minutes, Total Time: 30 minutes

tablespoons olive oil
1 large onion
1 red bell pepper
3 cloves garlic
1 teaspoon cumin
1 teaspoon paprika

1/2 teaspoon chili
powder
1 can tomatoes
Salt and black pepper
6 large eggs
1/4 cup fresh parsley

1. Heat olive oil in a large skillet over medium heat. Add the onion and bell pepper, sautéing until the vegetables are soft and golden, about 5-7 minutes. Add garlic, cumin, paprika, and chili powder.
2. Pour the crushed tomatoes into the skillet and season with salt and pepper. Let the sauce simmer for 10 minutes.
3. Add small wells in the sauce and add an egg to each well. Cover the skillet and cook on low heat for about 10 minutes or until the eggs are cooked to your desired level of doneness.
4. Sprinkle chopped parsley, cilantro, and crumbled feta cheese over the top.
Per serving: Calories: 280 kcal, Protein: 15 g, Carbohydrates: 20 g, Fat: 17 g, Fiber: 4 g, Cholesterol: 280 mg, Sodium: 400 mg.

POACHED EGGS ON WHOLE GRAIN TOAST WITH AVOCADO

Servings: 2, Prep Time: 10 minutes, Cook Time: 10 minutes, Total Time: 20 minutes

2 large eggs
2 slices whole grain
bread
1 ripe avocado
1 tsp lemon juice

Salt and black pepper
1 tbsp white vinegar (for
eggs)
1 tbsp olive oil
Fresh herbs

1. Halve the avocado, remove the pit, and scoop the flesh into a bowl. Add lemon juice, salt, and pepper. Mash with a fork until smooth.
2. Toast the whole grain bread slices until golden and crispy.
3. Fill a saucepan with water, add white vinegar, and gently simmer. Crack each egg into a small cup and gently pour into the simmering water. Cook for 3-4 minutes until the whites are set.
4. Spread the mashed avocado evenly on each slice of toast. Place a poached egg on top of each. Drizzle with olive oil and sprinkle with chili flakes and fresh herbs.
Per serving: Calories: 350 kcal, Protein: 13 g, Carbohydrates: 28 g, Fat: 22 g, Fiber: 8 g, Cholesterol: 185 mg, Sodium: 300 mg, Potassium: 600 mg

MUESLI WITH SKIM MILK AND FRESH BERRIES

Servings: 4, Prep Time: 10 minutes, Total Time: 10 minutes (plus optional overnight soaking)

2 cups rolled oats
1/4 cup sliced almonds
1/4 cup walnuts
2 tbsp sunflower seeds
2 tbsp pumpkin seeds
2 tbsp chia seeds

1/4 cup dried
cranberries or raisins
4 cups skim milk
1 tsp cinnamon
1 cup fresh berries

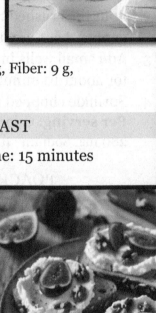

1. In a large mixing bowl, mix oats, almonds, walnuts, sunflower seeds, pumpkin seeds, chia seeds, and dried cranberries.
2. Pour skim milk over the mixture and sprinkle with cinnamon. Stir well. Cover and refrigerate overnight (or soak for at least 30 minutes).
3. Rinse fresh berries and set aside.
   Per serving: Calories: 350 kcal, Protein: 15 g, Carbohydrates: 50 g, Fat: 10 g, Fiber: 9 g, Cholesterol: 2 mg, Sodium: 80 mg, Potassium: 300 mg

RICOTTA AND FIG SPREAD ON WHOLE GRAIN TOAST

Servings: 4, Prep Time: 10 minutes, Cook Time: 5 minutes, Total Time: 15 minutes

4 slices whole grain bread
1 cup ricotta cheese
6 fresh figs, sliced
1/4 tsp ground cinnamon
Fresh mint leaves, for garnish

1. Toast the whole grain bread slices until golden and crispy.
2. Mix ricotta cheese with cinnamon and lemon zest until smooth in a bowl.
3. Spread the ricotta mixture on each slice of toasted bread. Top with sliced figs or spread with fig jam. Add chopped walnuts and drizzle with honey if desired.
4. Garnish each toast with fresh mint leaves. Serve immediately.
   Per serving: Calories: 250 kcal, Protein: 10 g, Carbohydrates: 35 g, Fat: 9 g, Fiber: 5 g, Cholesterol: 20 mg, Sodium: 200 mg.

GREEK YOGURT WITH HONEY AND NUTS

Servings: 2 servings, Prep Time: 5 minutes, Cook Time: 0 minutes, Total Time: 5 minutes

1 cup Greek yogurt
2 tablespoons honey
1/4 cup mixed nuts
Optional: Fresh berries or fruit slices for topping

1. Using whole nuts, roughly chop them to your desired size. This helps release their oils and flavors.
2. Divide the Greek yogurt between two serving bowls. Drizzle each bowl with honey, adjusting more or less according to your sweetness preference. Sprinkle the chopped nuts over the yogurt.
Per serving: Calories: 280 kcal, Protein: 15 g, Carbohydrates: 20 g, Fat: 15 g, Fiber: 2 g, Cholesterol: 10 mg, Sodium: 50 mg.

MEDITERRANEAN OMELETTE

Servings: 2 servings, Prep Time: 10 minutes, Cook Time: 10 minutes, Total Time: 20 minutes

4 large eggs
2 tablespoons olive oil
1/4 cup red onion, finely chopped
1/2 cup bell pepper
1/4 cup black olives

1 medium tomato
1/4 cup feta cheese
1 tablespoon parsley
1 teaspoon dried oregano
Salt and black pepper

1. Heat 1 tablespoon of olive oil in a non-stick skillet. Sauté the onion and bell pepper until soft, about 3-4 minutes. Add the tomatoes and olives, and cook for 2 minutes.
2. Whisk the eggs with oregano, salt, and pepper in a bowl. Heat the remaining olive oil. Pour in the egg mixture. As the eggs start to set, gently lift the edges with a spatula.
3. Once the eggs are mostly set but slightly runny on top, sprinkle the sautéed vegetables evenly over one-half of the omelet. Add the spinach or arugula if using, and sprinkle with feta cheese.
4. Carefully fold the other half of the omelet over the filled half. Let it cook for 1-2 minutes.
Per serving: Calories: 350 kcal, Protein: 21 g, Carbohydrates: 9 g, Fat: 27 g, Fiber: 2 g, Cholesterol: 372 mg, Sodium: 560 mg.

FUL MEDAMES

Servings: 4, Prep Time: 10 minutes, Cook Time: 1 hour, Total Time: 1 hour 10 minutes

cups dried fava
beans, soaked
overnight
4 cups water
3 cloves garlic
1/4 cup lemon juice
1/4 cup olive oil

1 tsp ground cumin
Salt and pepper
1 small red onion
1/4 cup fresh parsley
2 tomatoes

1. Drain the soaked beans and place them in a large pot with 4 cups of water. Bring to a boil, reduce heat to low, cover, and simmer for about 1 hour until tender. Skim off any foam.
2. In a small bowl, mix garlic, lemon juice, olive oil, cumin, salt, and pepper to create a dressing.
3. Drain the beans, reserving some cooking liquid. Mash the beans coarsely in the pot.
4. Stir the garlic-lemon dressing into the mashed beans. Mix in onions, parsley, and tomatoes. Add chili if using.
   Per serving: Calories: 290 kcal, Protein: 15 g, Carbohydrates: 40 g, Fat: 10 g, Fiber: 10 g, Cholesterol: 0 mg, Sodium: 300 mg.

BANANA OAT PANCAKES

Servings: 4 (about 8 pancakes), Prep Time: 10 minutes, Cook Time: 15 minutes, Total Time: 25 minutes

2 ripe bananas
1 cup rolled oats
2 large eggs
1/2 cup milk
1 tsp vanilla extract

1/2 tsp cinnamon
1 tsp baking powder
Pinch of salt
Butter or oil for
cooking

1. Combine bananas, oats, eggs, milk, vanilla, cinnamon, baking powder, and salt in a blender until smooth.
2. Warm a non-stick skillet over medium heat.
3. Pour 1/4 cup of batter per pancake onto the skillet. Cook for 2-3 minutes until edges firm up and bubbles form, then flip and cook for another 2-3 minutes until golden.
4. Enjoy hot with toppings like maple syrup and fresh banana slices.
   Per serving: Calories: 220, Protein: 7 g, Carbohydrates: 36 g, Fat: 6 g, Fiber: 4g.

BANANA MUFFINS

Servings: 12 muffins, Prep Time: 15 minutes, Cook Time: 20 minutes, Total Time: 35 minutes

3 ripe bananas, mashed
3/4 cup sugar
1 egg
1/3 cup melted butter
1 1/2 cups flour

1 tsp baking soda
1 tsp baking powder
1/2 tsp salt
Optional: 1/2 cup chocolate chips or nuts

1. Set to 375°F (190°C). Line a muffin tin with paper liners.
2. In a bowl, combine bananas, sugar, egg, and melted butter. In another bowl, mix flour, baking soda, baking powder, and salt.
3. Add the dry and wet ingredients, stirring until just combined.
4. Spoon batter into muffin cups, filling each about two-thirds full. Bake for 20 minutes or until a toothpick inserted comes out clean.
5. Let muffins cool in the pan for 5 minutes, then transfer to a wire rack.
Per muffin: Calories: 190, Protein: 2g, Carbohydrates: 30g, Fat: 7g, Fiber: 1g, Cholesterol: 25mg, Sodium: 200mg.

CHOCOLATE CHIA PUDDING

Servings: 4, Prep Time: 10 minutes, Chill Time: 4 hours, Total Time: 4 hours 10 minutes

1/4 cup cocoa powder
2 tbsp honey or maple syrup
1/2 tsp vanilla extract

Pinch of salt
1/3 cup chia seeds
2 cups milk

1. Combine cocoa powder, honey (or maple syrup), vanilla extract, and salt in a mixing bowl.
2. Stir in chia seeds until evenly distributed.
3. Gradually add milk, whisking to ensure the mixture is smooth.
4. Cover the bowl and refrigerate for at least 4 hours until the pudding thickens and the chia seeds have absorbed the liquid.
5. Stir the pudding before serving. Optional toppings include whipped cream, berries, or chocolate shavings for added flavor and decoration.
Per serving: Calories: 180, Protein: 6g, Carbohydrates: 25g, Fat: 8g, Fiber: 10g

MENEMEN

Servings: 4, Prep Time: 10 minutes, Cook Time: 20 minutes, Total Time: 30 minutes

2 tbsp olive oil	6 large eggs
1 large onion	1 tsp paprika
2 bell peppers	Salt and pepper
2 cloves garlic	1/4 cup fresh parsley
4 large tomatoes	

1. Heat olive oil in a large skillet. Add onions and bell peppers; cook until soft. Add garlic; cook for another minute.
2. Incorporate tomatoes, paprika, and cumin, seasoning with salt and pepper. Simmer about 10 minutes.
3. Crack eggs directly into the skillet. Let them set slightly, then scramble gently into the tomato mixture.
4. Stir in parsley. If using, top with crumbled feta and chili flakes.
   Per serving: Calories: 260 kcal, Protein: 15 g, Carbohydrates: 15 g, Fat: 17 g, Fiber: 3 g, Cholesterol: 280 mg, Sodium: 350 mg.

ITALIAN FRITTATA

Servings: 4 servings, Prep Time: 15 minutes, Cook Time: 25 minutes, Total Time: 40 minutes

6 large eggs	1 red bell pepper
1/4 cup milk	2 cloves garlic
salt and pepper	1 cup fresh spinach
2 tablespoons olive oil	1/2 cup cherry tomatoes
1 onion	1/4 cup fresh basil

1. Preheat the oven to 375°F (190°C).
2. Whisk together eggs, milk, salt, and pepper in a bowl. Set aside.
3. Heat olive oil in an oven-safe skillet over medium heat. Sauté onion and red bell pepper until softened, about 5 minutes. Add garlic and cook for another minute. Stir in spinach and cook until wilted.
4. Pour the egg mixture over the vegetables. Cook for about 3-4 minutes until the edges begin to set.
5. Sprinkle cherry tomatoes, basil, and parmesan cheese over the top.
6. Transfer the skillet to the preheated oven. Bake for 15-20 minutes.
   Per serving: Calories: 230 kcal, Protein: 14 g, Carbohydrates: 8 g, Fat: 16 g, Fiber: 2 g, Cholesterol: 280 mg, Sodium: 400 mg.

CAPRESE AVOCADO TOAST

Servings: 2, Prep Time: 10 minutes, Cook Time: 5 minutes, Total Time: 15 minutes

3 slices of whole-grain bread
1 large ripe avocado
1 small garlic clove, minced
Salt and pepper, to taste
1 large ripe tomato, sliced

4 oz fresh mozzarella cheese, sliced
1 tablespoon olive oil
Fresh basil leaves for garnish

1. Halve the avocado, remove the pit, and scoop the flesh into a bowl. Mash the avocado with the minced garlic, salt, and pepper until smooth.
2. Toast the whole-grain bread slices until golden and crisp.
3. Spread the mashed avocado evenly onto the toasted bread slices. Layer slices of fresh tomato and mozzarella cheese on top of the avocado. Drizzle with olive oil and, optionally, balsamic glaze for added flavor.

Per serving: Calories: 400 kcal, Protein: 18 g, Carbohydrates: 32 g, Fat: 25 g, Fiber: 7 g, Cholesterol: 45 mg, Sodium: 500 mg, Potassium: 600 mg.

LABNEH WITH OLIVE OIL AND ZA'ATAR

Servings: 4, Prep Time: 10 minutes (plus 12-24 hours for straining), Total Time: 10 minutes active, plus straining time

2 cups plain Greek yogurt
1/2 teaspoon salt
2 tablespoons olive oil
2 tablespoons za'atar
Fresh mint or parsley

1. Line a sieve with cheesecloth and place it over a bowl. Mix yogurt with salt and pour it into the sieve. Cover and refrigerate for 12-24 hours to drain.
2. Transfer thickened yogurt to a serving dish and create a shallow well in the center with the back of a spoon.
3. Drizzle olive oil over labneh.
4. Garnish with chopped mint or parsley. Serve with warm pita bread, cucumbers, or olives.

Per serving: Calories: 150 kcal, Protein: 9 g, Carbohydrates: 5 g, Fat: 11 g, Fiber: 1 g, Cholesterol: 10 mg, Sodium: 300 mg, Potassium: 120 mg

TORTILLA ESPAÑOLA

Servings: 4, Prep Time: 15 minutes, Cook Time: 25 minutes, Total Time: 40 minutes

4 large eggs
 1/2 cup olive oil
3 medium potatoes
1 large onion, thinly sliced
Salt and pepper, to taste

1. Heat olive oil in a skillet over medium heat. Add potatoes, onions, salt, and pepper. Cook until the potatoes are tender but not browned, about 10-15 minutes.
2. Whisk eggs with salt and pepper in a bowl. Drain potatoes and onions from oil and mix them into the eggs.
3. Remove excess oil from the skillet, leaving a thin layer. Pour the egg mixture back in, spreading evenly. Cook over low heat until mostly set, about 10 minutes.
4. Cover the skillet with the plate, invert both, and slide the tortilla back into the skillet. Cook the other side for 5 more minutes.
   Per serving: Calories: 300 kcal, Protein: 8 g, Carbohydrates: 20 g, Fat: 22 g, Fiber: 2 g, Cholesterol: 186 mg, Sodium: 200 mg, Potassium: 470 mg.

CILBIR (TURKISH POACHED EGGS WITH YOGURT)

Servings: 2, Prep Time: 5 minutes, Cook Time: 10 minutes, Total Time: 15 minutes

4 large eggs
1 cup plain Greek yogurt
1 clove garlic, minced
1 tbsp olive oil
1 tbsp white vinegar

2 tbsp unsalted butter
1 tsp smoked paprika
1/2 tsp red pepper flakes
Salt and pepper to taste
Fresh dill for garnish

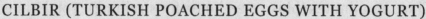

1. Combine yogurt, minced garlic, olive oil, salt, and pepper in a bowl. Spread evenly into two serving dishes.
2. Bring a pot of water with vinegar to a simmer. Gently drop in eggs and poach for 3-4 minutes until whites are set but yolks remain runny. Remove with a slotted spoon and drain.
3. Melt butter in a skillet, add paprika and red pepper flakes, and cook until fragrant, about 30 seconds.
4. Place two poached eggs on each yogurt bed, drizzle with spiced butter, and garnish with dill.
   Per serving: Calories: 450, Protein: 25g, Carbohydrates: 10g, Fats: 35g, Fiber: 1g, Cholesterol: 370mg, Sodium: 300mg, Potassium: 300mg
5.

PISTACHIO AND ROSE WATER OATMEAL

Servings: 2, Prep Time: 5 minutes, Cook Time: 10 minutes, Total Time: 15 minutes

1 cup rolled oats
2 cups water or milk
1/4 teaspoon salt
2 tablespoons pistachios
1 tablespoon rose water

1 tablespoon honey or
maple syrup
1/4 teaspoon ground
cardamon

1. Bring water or milk to a boil in a medium saucepan. Add the rolled oats and salt, reducing the heat to a simmer.
2. Cook the oats, stirring occasionally, until they have absorbed the liquid and reached your desired consistency, about 5-7 minutes.
3. Once the oats are cooked, stir in the rose water, honey or maple syrup, and ground cardamom. Mix well to combine all flavors.
   Per serving: Calories: 250 kcal, Protein: 6 g, Carbohydrates: 38 g, Fat: 9 g, Fiber: 5 g, Cholesterol: 0 mg, Sodium: 300 mg, Potassium: 200 mg

SIMIT

Servings: 8, Prep Time: 20 minutes, Rising Time: 1 hour 30 minutes, Cook Time: 20 minutes, Total Time: About 2 hours 10 minutes

2 cups whole-grain flour
2 cups all-purpose flour
1 tsp salt
1 tbsp instant yeast
1 tbsp sugar
1 1/4 cups warm water

1/4 cup vegetable oil
1/2 cup molasses
1/2 cup water (for molasses
bath)
1 cup sesame seeds

1. Mix the flour, salt, sugar, and yeast. Add warm water and oil and mix to form a dough. Knead for 10 minutes, then let rise for 1 hour.
2. Divide the risen dough into 8 pieces. Roll each into a 20-inch rope, form a circle, twist ends, and seal.
3. Mix molasses with water in one dish and place sesame seeds in another. Dip each dough ring in the molasses mixture and coat with sesame seeds.
4. Place on a baking sheet and rest for 30 minutes. Bake at 400°F for 20 minutes.
   Per servings: Calories: 320 kcal, Protein: 9 g, Carbohydrates: 53 g, Fat: 8 g, Fiber: 4 g.

BARLEY PORRIDGE

Servings: 4 servings, Prep Time: 5 minutes, Cook Time: 30 minutes, Total Time: 35 minutes

1 cup pearl barley
4 cups water or milk
1/4 teaspoon salt
2 tablespoons honey or

maple syrup
1/2 teaspoon cinnamon
1/4 cup chopped nuts
1/2 cup fresh berries

1. Combine rinsed barley, water or milk, and salt in a saucepan and bring to a boil. Reduce the heat to low, cover, and simmer for 25-30 minutes. Stir occasionally to prevent sticking.
2. Once the barley is cooked, stir in honey or maple syrup and cinnamon. Mix well to combine.
3. Serve warm with additional honey or maple syrup.
   Per serving: Calories: 280 kcal, Protein: 6 g, Carbohydrates: 55 g, Fat: 5 g, Fiber: 9 g, Cholesterol: 0 mg, Sodium: 150 mg, Potassium: 200 mg

GREEK YOGURT BERRY SMOOTHIE

Servings: 2, Prep Time: 5 minutes, Cook Time: 0 minutes, Total Time: 5 minutes

1 cup Greek yogurt
1 cup mixed berries
1 banana, sliced
1/2 cup almond milk
1 tablespoon honey
1/2 teaspoon vanilla extract

1. If using fresh berries, wash and prepare them.
2. Combine Greek yogurt, mixed berries, banana, almond milk, honey, and vanilla extract in a blender. If using chia seeds or flaxseeds, add them as well. Blend on high until smooth. If the smoothie is too thick, add more milk to reach your desired consistency. If it is too thin, add more berries.
3. Pour the smoothie into glasses and serve immediately for the freshest flavor.
   Per serving: Calories: 220 kcal, Protein: 12 g, Carbohydrates: 36 g, Fat: 4 g, Fiber: 4 g, Cholesterol: 5 mg, Sodium: 55 mg, Potassium: 350 mg

DESSERTS

TIRAMISU

Servings: 8, Prep Time: 30 minutes, Chill Time: 4 hours or overnight, Total Time: 4 hours 30 minutes

3 large eggs
1/4 cup honey
1 cup mascarpone cheese
1 cup Greek yogurt
1 cup strong brewed coffee

1/2 cup almond milk
1 teaspoon vanilla extract
24 wheat ladyfingers
1 tablespoon cocoa powder

1. Whisk egg yolks and honey until thick. Incorporate mascarpone and Greek yogurt until smooth.
2. Beat whites to stiff peaks and fold into the mascarpone mixture.
3. Combine coffee, milk, and vanilla.
4. Dip ladyfingers briefly in a coffee mixture and lay them in a dish. Cover with half the mascarpone mix, add another layer of dipped ladyfingers, and top with the mascarpone.
5. Refrigerate covered for 4 hours or overnight.
6. Dust with cocoa powder and sprinkle with cinnamon before serving.
   Per serving: Calories: 280 kcal, Protein: 9 g, Carbs: 35 g, Fat: 12 g, Fiber: 1 g

BAKLAVA

Servings: 20 pieces, Prep Time: 30 minutes, Cook Time: 50 minutes, Total Time: 1 hour 20 minutes

1/2 lb phyllo dough
2 cups mixed nuts
1/4 cup honey
1/4 cup olive oil
1 teaspoon cinnamon
1/2 teaspoon

cardamom
For the syrup:
1/2 cup honey
1/2 cup water
1/4 cup lemon juice
1 cinnamon stick

1. Preheat the oven to 350°F (175°C). Brush a baking dish with olive oil. Lay one sheet of phyllo in the dish and brush it with olive oil.
2. Evenly spread the nut mixture over the layered phyllo.
1. Cut the baklava into diamond or square shapes before baking. Bake for about 50 minutes.
2. Combine 1/2 cup honey, water, lemon juice, and a cinnamon stick in a saucepan. Bring to a boil, then lower heat and simmer for 10 minutes. Remove the cinnamon stick.
3. When the baklava comes out of the oven, pour the warm honey syrup.
   Per serving: Calories: 220 kcal, Protein: 3 g, Carbohydrates: 24 g, Fat: 12 g, Fiber: 2 g, Cholesterol: 0 mg, Sodium: 120 mg, Potassium: 85 mg

RICOTTA AND LEMON CAKE

Servings: 8, Prep Time: 15 minutes, Cook Time: 35 minutes, Total Time: 50 minutes

1/2 cup all-purpose flour
2 tsp baking powder
1/2 tsp salt
3/4 cup sugar
Zest of 2 lemons

3 large eggs
1 cup ricotta cheese
1/2 tsp vanilla extract
1/2 cup olive oil
1/4 cup lemon juice

1. Preheat oven to 350°F (175°C). Grease and flour a pan.
2. Whisk flour, baking powder, and salt in a bowl.
3. Whisk sugar, lemon zest, and eggs until fluffy in another bowl. Mix in ricotta, vanilla, and olive oil until smooth
4. Gradually mix dry ingredients into wet until just combined. Stir in lemon juice.
5. Pour batter into prepared pan. Bake for 35 minutes or until a toothpick comes out clean.
6. Let cool in the pan for 10 minutes, then transfer to a rack and cool completely.
   Per serving: Calories: 320 kcal, Protein: 7 g, Carbs: 35 g, Fat: 18 g, Fiber: 1 g, Sodium: 220 mg

TURKISH DELIGHT

Servings: 36 pieces, Prep Time: 10 minutes, Cook Time: 1 hour, Setting Time: 6-8 hours, Total Time: About 7-9 hours

4 cups water
2 cups granulated sugar
1 teaspoon lemon juice
1 cup cornstarch

1 teaspoon cream of tartar
2 tablespoons rose water
1/4 cup chopped pistachios
Powdered sugar for dusting

1. Combine 1 cup water, sugar, and lemon juice in a saucepan. Boil and simmer for 15 minutes.
2. In another saucepan, mix 3 cups water with cornstarch and cream of tartar. Cook over low heat, stirring until thick.
3. Gradually add the sugar syrup to the cornstarch mixture, stirring continuously. Cook for 45-60 minutes.
4. Stir in rose water, pistachios, cardamom.
5. Pour into a greased 8x8-inch pan dusted with cornstarch. Allow to cool, then cover and set for 6-8 hours.
6. Cut into squares and dust with powdered sugar.
   Per piece: Calories: 100 kcal, Protein: 0.5 g, Carbohydrates: 22 g, Fat: 1 g

BLUEBERRY PANNA COTTA

Servings:4, Preparation Time: 10 minutes, Cooking Time: 10 minutes, Total Time: 20 minutes active, 4 hours inactive

2 cups fresh blueberries
1/4 cup water
1/4 cup honey
1 teaspoon lemon zest
1 tablespoon lemon juice
1/2 teaspoons gelatin powder
1/2 tablespoons cold water
1/2 cups plain Greek yogurt

1. Combine blueberries, 1/4 cup water, honey, lemon zest, and lemon juice over medium heat. Cook until the blueberries begin to burst and the sauce thickens slightly about 5-7 minutes.
2. Sprinkle gelatin over 2 tablespoons of cold water in a small bowl. Let it sit for 5-10 minutes to bloom.
3. Transfer the blueberry mixture to a blender and puree until smooth.
4. If the blueberry mixture has cooled, slightly reheat it. Add the bloomed gelatin to the warm blueberry mixture and stir until completely dissolved.
5. Whisk together the Greek yogurt and milk. Gradually whisk in the blueberry and gelatin.
6. Divide the mixture into serving glasses or molds. Refrigerate for at least 4 hours or until set.
7. Garnish with fresh blueberries and a sprig of mint before serving.
   Per serving: Calories: 180 kcal, Protein: 8 g, Carbohydrates: 28 g, Fats: 3 g, Fiber: 2 g, Cholesterol: 10 mg, Sodium: 50 mg

RICE PUDDING

Servings: 6, Prep Time: 10 minutes, Cook Time: 45 minutes, Total Time: 55 minutes

1 cup brown rice
4 cups almond milk
1/4 cup honey
1 cinnamon stick
1/4 teaspoon salt
1/2 teaspoon vanilla extract
Zest one lemon
1/4 cup chopped almonds

1. Combine rice, almond milk, cinnamon sticks, and salt in a saucepan. Boil, then simmer for 40-45 minutes.
2. Remove cinnamon and mix in honey/maple syrup, vanilla, and raisins. Cook for 5 more minutes until thickened.
3. Stir in lemon zest. Serve warm or chilled, garnished with nuts.
   Per serving: Calories: 250 kcal, Protein: 5 g, Carbohydrates: 45 g, Fat: 6 g, Fiber: 3 g, Sodium: 150 mg

CANNOLI

Servings: 12 cannoli, Prep Time: 30 minutes, Cook Time: 10 minutes, Total Time: 40 minutes + chilling

Shells:
1 cup whole wheat pastry flour
2 tbsp almond flour
1 tbsp sugar
1/4 tsp salt
1 tbsp unsalted butter
1/4 cup apple cider vinegar

Filling:
1 cup ricotta cheese, strained
1/4 cup powdered
1/2 tsp vanilla extract
1/4 tsp orange zest
Garnish:
Dark chocolate chips

1. Mix whole wheat and almond flour with sugar and salt. Work in butter until crumbly. Chill for 30 minutes.
2. Roll dough thin, cut into 4-inch circles, and wrap around cannoli molds. Deep fry or bake at 375°F for 10 minutes until golden. Cool and remove from molds.
3. Combine ricotta, powdered sugar, vanilla, and orange zest. Pipe into cooled shells.
4. Dip ends in chocolate or pistachios. Chill before serving.
   Per serving: Calories: 120 kcal, Protein: 4 g, Carbs: 15 g, Fat: 5 g, Fiber: 1 g

SORBETES

Servings: 6, Prep Time: 15 minutes, Freeze Time: 2 hours, Total Time: 2 hours 15 minutes

2 cups fresh fruit
1/2 cup water
1/3 cup honey or maple syrup
1 tbsp lemon juice
Pinch of salt
Wash, prepare, and puree the fruit in a blender until smooth.

1. Combine water and honey/maple syrup in a saucepan. Boil and simmer for 5 minutes. Cool slightly.
2. In a bowl, mix the fruit puree, syrup, lemon juice, salt, and optional mint or basil.
3. Refrigerate the mixture for at least 1 hour until cold.
4. Churn in an ice cream maker according to the manufacturer's instructions, then transfer to a container and freeze for another 1-2 hours for a firmer texture.
5. Garnish with fresh mint or fruit if desired.
   Per serving: Calories: 120 kcal, Protein: 1 g, Carbohydrates: 30 g, Fat: 0 g, Fiber: 2 g

STUFFED ZUCCHINI FLOWERS

Servings:4, Preparation Time: 15 minutes, Cooking Time:, 10 minutes, Total Time: 25 minutes

For the Filling:
8 zucchini flowers
1 cup ricotta cheese
1/4 cup parmesan cheese
1 egg, lightly beaten
1 tablespoon fresh basil

1 tablespoon fresh mint
Zest of 1 lemon
Salt and pepper
For Cooking:
2 tablespoons olive oil
1 garlic clove

1. Open the zucchini flowers and remove the stamens. Rinse carefully and pat dry.
2. Mix ricotta, parmesan, beaten egg, basil, mint, lemon zest, salt, and pepper until well combined.
3. Carefully spoon the cheese into each zucchini flower. Twist the tips of the petals to close and secure the filling inside.
4. Heat olive oil in a skillet over medium heat. Add minced garlic and sauté for about 1 minute until fragrant. Place the stuffed flowers in the skillet and cook for 2 minutes per side.
5. Serve the stuffed zucchini flowers warm or without tomato sauce.
   Per serving: Calories: 200 kcal, Protein: 12 g, Carbohydrates: 6 g, Fats: 14 g, Fiber: 1 g, Cholesterol: 65 mg, Sodium: 300 mg, Potassium: 200 mg

FIG AND HONEY GLAZED CHICKEN

Servings: 4, Prep Time: 15 minutes, Cook Time: 30 minutes, Total Time: 45 minutes

4 chicken breasts
2 tablespoons olive oil
6 fresh figs, diced
3 tablespoons honey
2 tablespoons balsamic

vinegar
1 clove garlic
1 teaspoon fresh thyme
Salt and black pepper
Fresh fig slices for garnish

1. Pat the chicken dry and season with salt and pepper. Heat olive oil in a skillet. Sear the chicken for 6-7 minutes on each side.
2. Add diced figs, honey, balsamic vinegar, garlic, thyme, and red pepper flakes in the same skillet. Cook over medium heat for 5 minutes.
3. Return the chicken to the skillet, spooning the fig and honey glaze over the top. Cook for 5 more minutes (internal temperature of 165°F).
4. Garnish with fresh fig slices and a sprinkle of crumbled cheese if desired.
   Per serving: Calories: 350 kcal, Protein: 26 g, Carbohydrates: 24 g, Fats: 14 g, Fiber: 3 g, Cholesterol: 65 mg, Sodium: 200 mg, Potassium: 400 mg

ROASTED PEPPER AND ARTICHOKE ANTIPASTO

Servings: 6, Preparation Time: 15 minutes, Cooking Time: 25 minutes, Total Time: 40 minutes

3 bell peppers
1 can artichoke hearts
1/4 cup olive oil
2 tablespoons capers
3 cloves garlic, minced
1/2 cup Kalamata olives

2 tablespoons balsamic vinegar
1 teaspoon Italian herbs
Salt and black pepper
1/4 cup fresh basil
1/4 cup fresh parsley

1. Preheat your oven to 425°F (220°C).
2. Toss the sliced bell peppers and artichoke hearts with olive oil, salt, and pepper on a large baking sheet.
3. Roast in the oven for 20-25 minutes until the peppers are soft.
4. Combine the roasted peppers, artichokes, capers, minced garlic, olives, balsamic vinegar, and Italian herbs.
5. Stir in the fresh basil, parsley, and lemon zest before serving.
   Per serving: Calories: 150 kcal, Protein: 2 g, Carbohydrates: 10 g, Fats: 12 g, Fiber: 4 g, Cholesterol: 0 mg, Sodium: 300 mg, Potassium: 250 mg

WINTER CITRUS SALAD WITH FENNEL AND POMEGRANATE

Servings: 4, Prep Time: 15 minutes, Total Time: 15 minutes

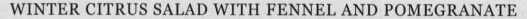

4 large oranges
1 grapefruit
1 small fennel bulb
1/2 cup pomegranate seeds
1/4 cup red onion
1/4 cup fresh mint leaves

1/4 cup fresh parsley
3 tablespoons olive oil
2 tablespoons lemon juice
Salt and black pepper
Mixed greens

1. Segment the oranges and grapefruit, capturing any juice for the dressing.
2. Whisk together citrus, olive oil, lemon juice, and honey. Season with salt and pepper.
3. Combine citrus segments, fennel, red onion, pomegranate seeds, mint, and parsley in a bowl. Toss with dressing.
4. Place mixed greens on plates, top with salad, and serve immediately.
   Per serving: Calories: 180 kcal, Protein: 2 g, Carbohydrates: 25 g, Fat: 10 g, Fiber: 5 g, Sodium: 50 mg

WINTER SQUASH AND SAGE RISOTTO

Servings: 4, Prep Time: 15 minutes, Cook Time: 30 minutes, Total Time: 45 minutes

1 tablespoon olive oil
1 small onion
2 cloves garlic
1 cup arborio rice
4 cups vegetable broth
2 cups butternut squash

1 tablespoon fresh sage
1/4 cup grated parmesan
cheese
Salt and black pepper
2 tablespoons unsalted
butter

1. Preheat oven to 400°F. Toss squash with oil, salt, and pepper. Roast for 20 minutes until tender.
2. Heat olive oil in a skillet over medium heat. Sauté onion and garlic until soft. Add rice, stirring until the edges are translucent. Gradually add broth, one ladle at a time, allowing each addition to absorb before adding the next, until rice is creamy and al dente, for 18-20 minutes.
3. Stir in roasted squash, sage, parmesan, and butter—season with salt and pepper.

Per serving: Calories: 380 kcal, Protein: 9 g, Carbohydrates: 53 g, Fats: 14 g, Fiber: 3 g, Cholesterol: 15 mg, Sodium: 600 mg, Potassium: 300 mg

CRANBERRY AND PISTACHIO COUSCOUS SALAD

Servings: 4 servings, Preparation Time: 15 minutes, Cooking Time: 5 minutes, Total Time: 20 minutes

1 cup couscous
1 1/4 cups boiling water
1/3 cup dried
cranberries (pistachio)
1/3 cup pistachios
1/4 cup fresh parsley

1/4 cup fresh mint
3 tablespoons olive oil
Juice and zest of 1 lemon
1 small red onion
Salt and black pepper

1. Place the couscous in a large heatproof bowl. Pour the boiling water over the couscous and cover the bowl with. Let it sit for 5 minutes, then fluff it with a fork.
2. Add the cranberries, pistachios, onion, and parsley to the couscous.
3. Whisk the olive oil, lemon juice, lemon zest, salt, black pepper, and optional red pepper flakes. Pour the dressing over the couscous mixture and toss until coated.
4. Let the salad sit for 10 minutes to allow the flavors to meld together.

Per serving: Calories: 330 kcal, Protein: 8 g, Carbohydrates: 45 g, Fats: 14 g, Fiber: 6 g, Cholesterol: 0 mg, Sodium: 10 mg, Potassium: 290 mg

TZATZIKI SAUCE

Servings: 6, Prep Time: 15 minutes, Total Time: 15 minutes (plus optional chilling)

2 cups Greek yogurt
1 large cucumber
2 cloves garlic
2 tablespoons fresh mint

Juice of 1 lemon
1 tablespoon olive oil
Salt and black pepper

1. Grate the cucumber, wrap it in a kitchen towel, and squeeze out excess water.
2. Combine Greek yogurt, grated cucumber, garlic, mint, lemon juice, olive oil, optional dill and lemon zest.
3. Season with salt and pepper to taste. For the best flavor, refrigerate for at least one hour before serving.
   Per serving: Calories: 70 kcal, Protein: 4 g, Carbohydrates: 3 g, Fats: 4 g, Fiber: 0.5 g, Cholesterol: 10 mg, Sodium: 50 mg, Potassium: 60 mg

MUHAMMARA: SPICY ROASTED RED PEPPER AND WALNUT DIP

Servings: 6, Prep Time: 20 minutes, Cook Time: 10 minutes, Total Time: 30 minutes

3 large red bell peppers
1 cup walnuts, toasted
1/4 cup whole wheat breadcrumbs
2 cloves garlic, minced
2 tablespoons olive oil
1 tablespoon pomegranate molasses

1 teaspoon ground cumin
1/2 teaspoon smoked paprika
1/4 teaspoon cayenne pepper
Salt, to taste
Juice of 1 lemon

1. If using fresh peppers, roast in a 450°F oven until charred, about 15-20 minutes. Peel after cooling.
2. Toast in a skillet over medium heat until fragrant, about 5-7 minutes.
3. In a food processor, combine all ingredients except for the garnish. Blend until smooth.
4. Adjust salt and add lemon juice. Blend again.
5. Chill for at least 1 hour. Serve garnished with herbs if desired.
   Per serving: Calories: 220 kcal, Protein: 4 g, Carbohydrates: 12 g, Fat: 18 g, Fiber: 3 g, Sodium: 150 mg

BABA GANOUSH: SMOKY EGGPLANT DIP

Servings: 6, Prep Time: 10 minutes, Cook Time: 40 minutes, Total Time: 50 minutes

2 medium eggplants
3 tablespoons tahini
2 cloves garlic
Juice of 1 lemon

2 tablespoons olive oil
Salt and pepper
1/2 teaspoon cumin

1. Preheat the oven to 400°F (200°C). Prick the eggplants with a fork, place them on a baking sheet, and roast until tender for 40 minutes. Let them cool, peel off the skin, and scoop out the flesh.
2. In a food processor, combine eggplant flesh, tahini, garlic, lemon juice, olive oil, and cumin. Process until smooth. Season with salt, pepper, and optional smoked paprika.
3. Refrigerate for at least 1 hour.
4. Garnish with parsley and drizzle with olive oil if desired.
   Per serving: Calories: 120 kcal, Protein: 2 g, Carbohydrates: 13 g, Fat: 7 g, Fiber: 5 g, Sodium: 50 mg

ROMESCO SAUCE

Servings: 6 servings, Preparation Time, 10 minutes, Cooking Time: 20 minutes, Total Time: 30 minutes

4 large red bell peppers
1 medium tomato
1/2 cup whole almonds
2 cloves garlic
1/4 cup olive oil

2 tablespoons sherry vinegar
1 teaspoon smoked paprika
Salt and black pepper

1. Preheat your oven to 425°F (220°C). Place the bell peppers and tomato halves on a baking sheet, and add garlic cloves. Roast in the oven for 20 minutes. Remove them from the oven, cover them with aluminum foil for 10 minutes to steam, and peel off the skins.
2. Squeeze the garlic out of its skin. Remove the cores and seeds from the peppers.
3. In a food processor, combine the roasted peppers, tomato, peeled garlic, toasted almonds, olive oil, vinegar, smoked paprika, and cayenne pepper. Process until the mixture becomes a smooth sauce.
   Per serving: Calories: 200 kcal, Protein: 3 g, Carbohydrates: 9 g, Fats: 18 g, Fiber: 3 g, Cholesterol: 0 mg, Sodium: 150 mg, Potassium: 300 mg
4.

HOMEMADE TOMATO SAUCE

Servings:4 servings, Cooking Time: 30 minutes

2 pounds tomatoes
3 tablespoons olive oil
2 cloves garlic
1 small onion
1/4 cup fresh basil leaves
Salt and pepper

1. Peel (if desired) and chop the tomatoes. Mince the garlic and chop the onion finely.
2. Heat olive oil in a large skillet over medium heat. Add the garlic and onion, sautéing until translucent and fragrant, about 3-5 minutes.
3. Add the chopped tomatoes to the skillet—season with salt and pepper.
4. Reduce the heat to low and let the sauce simmer for 20-25 minutes, stirring occasionally, until it thickens and the flavors meld together.
5. Stir in the fresh basil for a few minutes before cooking the sauce.
6. Taste and adjust the seasoning with additional salt and pepper if needed.
   Per serving: Calories: 140 kcal, Protein: 2g, Carbohydrates: 10g, Fat: 10g, Fiber: 2g.

HOMEMADE RED BEET HUMMUS

Servings: 6 servings, Preparation Time: 15 minutes, Cooking Time: 1 hour (for roasting beets)

1 medium red beet
1 can chickpeas
1/4 cup tahini
2 tablespoons lemon juice

2 cloves garlic
2 tablespoons olive oil
1/2 teaspoon cumin
Salt to taste

1. Preheat your oven to 400°F (200°C). Wash the beet and wrap it in aluminum foil. Place on a baking sheet and roast in the oven for 45-60 minutes.
2. Combine the roasted beet, chickpeas, tahini, lemon juice, minced garlic, olive oil, cumin, and a pinch of salt. Blend until smooth.
3. Drizzle with olive oil and sprinkle sesame seeds.
4. Serve with fresh vegetables, pita bread, or as part of a mezze platter.
   Per serving: Calories: 180 kcal, Protein: 6g, Carbohydrates: 20g, Fats: 10g, Fiber: 5g, Cholesterol: 0 mg, Sodium: 300 mg.

SHOPPING-LIST WEEK 1

Dairy & Eggs
Greek yogurt, Feta cheese, Cottage cheese, Almond milk, Eggs

Fruits & Vegetables
Honey, Walnuts, Bananas, Cinnamon, Spinach, Tomatoes, Blueberries, Strawberries, Mango, Coconut flakes, Pineapple, Cherry tomatoes, Cucumbers, Olives, Avocado, Bell peppers, Asparagus, Baby Potatoes, Broccoli, Sweet potato, Mixed greens (for salad), Lemons, Garlic, Carrot sticks, Peach, Raisins, Cucumber, Apple, Pear, Pistachios, Bell pepper slices, Orange,

Sunflower seeds

Grains & Breads
Oatmeal, bread, tortillas, Brown rice, Spaghetti, Barley, pita

Proteins
Quinoa, Lentils, Chickpeas, Turkey, Chicken (for kebabs and grilled), Cod, Tofu, Shrimp, Tuna

Condiments & Extras
Hummus, Tzatziki sauce, Marinara sauce, Guacamole, Almond butter, Chia seeds

Nuts & Seeds
Almonds, unsweetened nuts

MEAL-PLAN WEEK 1

	Monday	Tuesday	Wednesday	Thursday	Friday	Saturday	Sunday
Breakfast	Greek yogurt with honey and walnuts.	Oatmeal with sliced bananas and a sprinkle of cinnamon	Two scrambled eggs with spinach and tomatoes	Smoothie with spinach, blueberries, banana, and almond milk	Whole grain toast with almond butter and sliced strawberries	Chia pudding with mango and coconut flakes	Cottage cheese with fresh pineapple
Lunch	Quinoa salad with cherry tomatoes, cucumbers, feta cheese, and olives	Lentil soup with whole-grain bread	Chickpea and avocado salad	Turkey and avocado wrap with whole grain tortilla	Greek salad with grilled chicken	Roasted vegetable and quinoa bowl	Mediterranean tuna salad served over mixed greens
Dinner	Grilled salmon with a side of asparagus	Chicken kebabs with mixed bell peppers	Baked cod with broccoli and sweet potato	Vegetable stir-fry and a side of brown rice	Spaghetti with marinara sauce and a side salad	Lemon-garlic shrimp over barley	Whole grain pita and a side of Greek salad
Snacks	A handful of almonds; carrot sticks with hummus	Greek yogurt, a peach	A small box of raisins, sliced cucumber	An apple, a handful of unsalted nuts	A pear; Greek yogurt with sliced almonds	A handful of pistachios	An orange, a handful of sunflower seeds

69

SHOPPING-LIST WEEK 2

Produce
Fresh figs, Whole grain bread, Avocados, Bananas, Pears, Lemons, Blueberries, Onions, Garlic, Potatoes, Red, yellow, and green bell peppers, Zucchini, Carrots, Tomatoes, Fennel bulb, Broccoli, Cucumbers, Fresh cherries, Oranges, Strawberries, Apples, Mixed berries

Dairy & Eggs
Ricotta cheese, Greek yogurt, Eggs, Cottage cheese, Feta cheese, Parmesan cheese, Butter

Meat & Seafood
Turkey breast cutlets, Fresh trout, Ground lamb, Shrimp, Pork loin, Pork belly, Chicken thighs, Chicken drumsticks, Sea bass fillets

Pantry & Dry Goods
Whole-grain toast, Almond butter, Olive oil, Honey, Oatmeal, Almonds, Spaghetti, Marinara sauce, Polenta, Saffron, Fish stock or vegetable broth, Dried lentils, Crushed tomatoes, Whole wheat couscous, Rice, Dried figs, Peanut butter, Guacamole

Herbs & Spices
Fresh parsley, Fresh mint, Fresh basil, Oregano, Paprika, Red pepper flakes, Cumin, Cardamom (optional), Ground cinnamon, Thyme, Rosemary, Dill, Sliced nuts (for oatmeal and snacking)

Snacks
Dried almonds, Walnuts

MEAL-PLAN WEEK 2

	Monday	Tuesday	Wednesday	Thursday	Friday	Saturday	Sunday
Breakfast	Ricotta and fig spread on whole-grain toast	Greek Yogurt Berry Smoothie	Poached Eggs on Toast with Avocado	Almond butter and banana toast on whole-grain bread	Shakshuka	Cottage cheese with sliced pears and honey	Oatmeal with almonds and blueberries
Lunch	Spaghetti with Marinara Sause	Potato Vegetable Hash	Lentil and Vegetable Stuffed Peppers	Fish Soup with Saffron	Broccoli and Feta Omelet	Greek salad	Stuffed tomatoes with rice and herbs
Dinner	Turkey meatballs in tomato sauce with polenta	Baked trout with Lemon and Herbs	Lamb Kofta	Porchetta	Spaghetti with marinara sauce and a side salad	Catalan Chicken	Baked sea bass with lemon and herbs
Snacks	Sliced apples with peanut butter	A handful of dried figs and almonds	Fresh cherries	Orange slices	Greek yogurt with sliced strawberries	Cucumber slices with guacamole	A small bowl of mixed berries

70

SHOPPING-LIST WEEK 3

Produce

Fresh berries (for multiple breakfasts), Barley, Bananas, Fresh spinach, Orzo, Red and yellow bell peppers, Tomatoes, Onions, Garlic, Fennel bulb, Fresh parsley, Fresh mint, Fresh basil, Oranges, Lemons, Apples, Peaches, Melon

Dairy & Eggs

Skim milk, Greek yogurt, Eggs (for French toast and Menemen), Cheese (various small servings), Cottage cheese, Protein powder (optional for a smoothie), Mozzarella cheese, Parmesan cheese

Meat & Seafood

Ground lamb (for cabbage rolls), Turkey breast cutlets, Lamb (for Arni Psito), Fresh sardines, Duck breasts

Pantry & Dry Goods

Muesli, Granola, Whole grain bread (for French toast and pizza crust), Honey, Whole grain pasta, Brown rice, Crushed tomatoes (for ratatouille and tomato soup), Chickpeas, Pine nuts, Walnuts, Whole grain crackers, Rosewater, Pistachios, Breadcrumbs

Canned & Jarred

Tuna (for Mediterranean tuna salad), Artichoke hearts, Roasted red peppers, Pomegranate juice (for duck sauce)

Herbs & Spices

Cumin, Smoked paprika, Dried herbs (like oregano and thyme), Fresh dill

Snacks & Drinks

Olives, Orange juice (for duck sauce)

MEAL-PLAN WEEK 3

	Monday	Tuesday	Wednesday	Thursday	Friday	Saturday	Sunday
Breakfast	Muesli with skim milk and fresh berries	Barley Porridge	Greek yogurt with granola and fresh berries	Pistachio and Rose Water Oatmeal	Berry and banana smoothie	French toast with whole grain bread and a side of honey	Menemen
Lunch	Tomato and Basil Soup	Mediterranean tuna salad	Spinach and orzo salad	Chickpea and roasted pepper wrap	Artichoke and spinach pizza on a whole-grain crust	Tabbouleh	Beetroot and walnut
Dinner	Ratatouille	Cabbage Rolls with Lamb and Rice	Moussaka	Pecan Crusted Turkey Gulets	Arni Psito	Baked Sardines	Duck breast with
Snacks	Sliced apples	dried figs	Fresh cherries	Orange slices	Greek yogurt	Cucumber slices	Mixed berries

71

SHOPPING-LIST WEEK 4

Produce
Avocados, Fresh figs, Pears, Bananas, Apples, Spinach, Arugula, Pomegranate seeds, Butternut squash, Tomatoes, Brussels sprouts, Asparagus, Lemons, Kiwi, Blueberries, Red onions, Garlic

Dairy & Eggs
Eggs, Ricotta cheese, Greek yogurt, Feta cheese, Cottage cheese, Mozzarella cheese

Meat & Seafood
Mackerel (for two dinners), Cod fillets, Chicken thighs, Shrimp, Trout

Herbs & Spices
Cinnamon, Thyme, Fresh basil

Grains & Bakery
Whole-grain bread (for toast and side), Whole-grain pita, Quinoa, Whole-grain pizza crust

Canned & Jarred
Olives, Capers, Crushed tomatoes (for tomato basil soup), Lentils, Black beans

Pantry & Dry Goods
Honey, Flax seeds, Tahini, Mixed seeds (like sunflower or pumpkin seeds), Trail mix ingredients (dried fruit, nuts, seeds), Almonds, Dried cranberries, Dark chocolate

Snacks
Peanut butter

MEAL-PLAN WEEK 4

	Monday	Tuesday	Wednesday	Thursday	Friday	Saturday	Sunday
Breakfast	Poached eggs on whole-grain toast with avocado	Ricotta and Fig Spread	Poached pear with cinnamon and Greek yogurt	Yogurt with mixed seeds	Spinach and feta breakfast wrap	Cottage cheese with sliced bananas	Green smoothie with spinach, apple
Lunch	Mediterranean falafel bowl with tahini dressing	Roasted butternut squash soup	Mediterranean platter with hummus, tabbouleh, and falafel	Tomato basil soup	Artichoke and Spinach Pizza on a Whole-Grain Crust	Lentil and vegetable stuffed peppers	Quinoa and black bean salad
Dinner	Grilled mackerel with a salad	Cod en papillote with tomatoes	Roasted chicken thighs with lemon and thyme	Garlic butter shrimp with a quinoa salad	Grilled mackerel with a side of mixed greens	Chicken with whole-grain pita	Baked trout
Snacks	Sliced apples with peanut butter	A handful of dried figs	Fresh cherries	Orange slices with s	Greek yogurt with sliced strawberries	Cucumber slices with guacamole	A small bowl of mixed berries

72

INDEX

Made in United States
Orlando, FL
01 October 2024

52188183R00043